ELITE
CHINA

LUXURY CONSUMER
BEHAVIOR IN CHINA

ELITE CHINA

LUXURY CONSUMER
BEHAVIOR IN CHINA

PIERRE XIAO LU

JOHN WILEY & SONS (ASIA) PTE. LTD.

Other Wiley Editorial Offices
John Wiley & Sons, Inc., 111 River Street, Hoboken, NJ 07030, USA
John Wiley & Sons Ltd, The Atrium, Southern Gate,
    Chichester PO19 BSQ, England
John Wiley & Sons (Canada) Ltd, 5353 Dundas Street West,
    Suite 400, Toronto, Ontario M9B 6H8, Canada
John Wiley & Sons Australia Ltd, 42 McDougall Street,
    Milton, Queensland 4064, Australia
Wiley-VCH, Boschstrasse 12, D-69469 Weinheim, Germany

Library of Congress Cataloging-in-Publication Data:
978-0-470-82267-8

Cover design and page layout by Alicia Beebe
Printed in Singapore by C.O.S. Printers Pte Ltd
10 9 8 7 6 5 4

To my wife, Qianqian

CONTENTS

ACKNOWLEDGMENTS

I WOULD LIKE to thank the following wonderful people who have given me enormous help in my research and without whom this book would not have been possible: Bernard Pras, André Fourçans, Dominique Xardel, Christian Koenig, Thierry Schwartz, Simon Nyeck, Michel Phan, Concetta Lanciaux, Emanuelle Le Nagard-Assayag, Hellmut Schütte, Denis Darpy, Christian Pinson, Raymond-Alain Thietart, Michel Chevalier, Michelle Chen, Lydie Liu, Hélène Zhang, Bei Zhang, Ming Zhao, and CJ Hwu.

T HE PAST 25 YEARS spent in assisting Bernard Arnault, CEO of LVMH, in the construction of the Group have given me a very special point of observation on the renewal of the luxury industry that has taken place in that period.

Indeed, in 1985, when we started integrating medium-sized luxury companies, mainly still held by families, luxury was moving from product to brand. Our task was to build local products into global brands.

Our focus was on enhancing the brands, rejuvenating them through the injection of global designers, and building an organization of excellence aligned with the quality, heritage and creativity of those brands.

During the first 15 years there was little concentration on customers in the luxury industry, since the accent was on creating desirability. However, thanks to the global retail networks, we have made luxury brands accessible to consumers as never before. And customers have become ultra-sophisticated, discerning, to the point where they are now at the center of the luxury industry and will remain there for years to come.

For this reason, Pierre Xiao Lu's book on Chinese consumer behavior is fundamental, because it challenges and overrides the perception that Chinese customers seek only the status aspect of luxury. As they become reacquainted with their refined luxury roots, Chinese consumers will embrace luxury as an entry to culture, to beauty, to the refined lifestyle they once had.

Modern Chinese elite is the core client of luxury. It is crucial to understand their value systems. Scanning their values from ancient China to today's communist planned market economy, Pierre Xiao-Lu presents an effective typology of Chinese luxury consumers, with characteristics of consumption for each segment: the luxury lovers, followers, intellectuals and laggards. Each segment has a different attitude toward brand loyalty, product innovation, and motivation to buy.

Pierre Xiao-Lu explores the geographical diversity that has an impact on consumer's behaviour. Being aware of the different approaches to luxury consumers in Beijing as opposed to Shanghai or other areas of China will give competitive advantage to a commercial strategy. He gives a striking demonstration of why and how Chinese luxury brands will be created for success, as Chinese are fast recuperating their ancient Chinese tradition of fine arts and craftsmanship.

Pierre Xiao Lu's vision is the one I had when I came to China in 1994 and fell in love with the evidence of its luxury tradition that I could still glimpse even then in busy Shanghai.

This book makes an important contribution to making China's past an integral part of building a future that remembers its luxury roots.

CONCETTA LANCIAUX, PHD
STRATEGY LUXURY ADVISOR, PARIS

Understand China's Elite, Understand China's Future

I N RECENT TIMES, there has been a great deal of media coverage of the "luxury fever" that is gripping China and how to sell luxury to the Chinese. But how well do you really understand Chinese luxury consumers?

Look closely at the photo of the Boutique Mont Blanc in the Champs-Elysees (*see photo section*). It shows a window display featuring Chinese-style decoration and calligraphy—a Chinese traditional stele with calligraphy against a golden background and two Chinese blue-and-white porcelains, sumptuously displayed with modern writing instruments made by Mont Blanc: a perfect combination of tradition and modernity, the Occidental and the Oriental.

Now look again. Can you see anything wrong in the picture? Perhaps not; but to anyone with a little understanding of Chinese language and culture the mistake will be obvious and a cause of undoubted mirth. The Chinese stele carefully fixed in the middle of the window was hung vertically, rather than horizontally, and thus unreadable.

The four Chinese characters (五世其昌, *wu shi qi chang*) mean the prosperity of five generations. The style of calligraphy is very forceful and solid, the gold indicating its origins in royal families or among aristocratic scholar-bureaucrats. (In imperial China, as in ancient Rome or ancient Egypt, the right to use this color in daily life was denied to ordinary people.)

Mont Blanc corrected the mistake very quickly. It has learned from this lesson and has gone on to develop a wonderful business in China's luxury market. And there is a lesson in this for everyone who wishes to do business in China: to be successful and to make your targeted Chinese clients happy requires some effort to get to know the market and the people living there. For most with such aspirations, their knowledge of the country is currently very limited; far less than they need. Many American and European companies, attracted by the country's rapid economic development and vast potential, have rushed in without taking the time to understand the market and are unprepared for what they find there. Access to the wallets of China's consumers is much harder to achieve than they think, especially for luxury brands.

The modern elite class in China has certain similar characteristics to those of its ancestors—the scholar-bureaucrats of ancient China. In this book, we set out to provide a clear guide to who they are, what they think, how they behave, what their attitudes toward luxury and luxury brands are, and the various differences among them.

In seeking to gain an understanding of the modern elite, we will examine aspects of luxury culture in ancient China and the social evolutions of Chinese society, addressing such issues as how a communist country has been so successful in developing a market-oriented economy and why the marketing and management of luxury have been remarkably effective here. In the process, we look at the relationships between social morality and the concept of luxury in modern China.

After clarifying these questions, we will focus on consumer value systems in today's China, which are crucial to an understanding of how to sell high-involvement products—in this case, fashion and luxury goods—in a market with such a strong cultural background. This, I hope, will help you to integrate all of this market knowledge into your branding strategy, consumer segmentation, selective retailing and merchandising, integrated marketing communication, and direct marketing, so that you can avoid mistakes and fit well in the market.

Then we go further to look closely at our luxury consumers. An effective typology of Chinese luxury consumers is introduced, with a detailed explanation of the characteristics of consumption of each segment, their value orientations and product design preferences, their geographic distribution, and suitable communication strategies to target the different segments. Some success stories are also discussed along the way.

In order to gain a more detailed picture of the whole Chinese market, we will take a business trip together to the main economic centers in the north, south, east, and central part of China to do some market visits. A profile of each of the main cities—its lifestyle, prevailing attitudes toward luxury, and all information necessary for conducting luxury business there—is presented and discussed.

The final chapter focuses on a very special issue: marketing strategies of Chinese luxury brands. In the first chapter, the reasons why there are no Chinese luxury brands in the booming Chinese luxury market are explained. This chapter introduces some step-by-step strategies for starting and developing brands, and illustrates these with case studies featuring successful Chinese or Chinese-related brands.

Finally, we integrate all that we have looked at to date into 10 marketing strategies which can be applied by both international and Chinese luxury brands in helping them to succeed in the Chinese market.

With the globalization of the world economy, the Chinese market is becoming of increasing strategic importance to multinational companies to ensure their long-term development. Economic development and internal changes in Chinese society are making people think and act differently from their predecessors. It is vital, therefore, for any company targeting affluent Chinese consumers to have a deeper understanding of the behavior of the Chinese elite, the leaders of Chinese society, who will shape the future of China. I believe that this book will help toward gaining that understanding.

"Love", 2007 Spring-Summer Collection of NE Tiger, a Chinese fashion brand.

Window display of Boutique Mont Blanc – Champs-Elysees, Paris, January 2004.

© Pierre Xiao Lu

Scholar-bureaucrats playing polo with the emperor, Tang dynasty

Polo as a luxury leisure and sports activity was very popular among the aristocrats and military generals in Tang, Song and Yuan dynasties. Many emperors and ministers were very good at this elite sport. It combines intelligence, techniques and strength.

Hunting as portrayed in "The Dream of The Red Chamber" by Cao Xueqin

Hunting was a way of leisure for the elite class of ancient Chinese society and reserved only for the aristocrat and scholar-bureaucrats. This young aristocrat is hunting to show that he has reached his manhood and can take on the responsibilities of working for the country.

Ladies (partial), Zhou Fang, Tang dynasty

The luxury and elegance can be clearly seen from the clothing and accessories of the lady in the painting. Her hair was carefully combed and sophisticatedly decorated with adornments and a fresh lotus. Her dress was very suitable and comfortable with pure cotton and high quality silks embroidered with colorful flowers. The exaggeration of the hairstyle and adornment showed the pursuit of extreme beauty and the fine art of life.

Xu Jinglei, actress and film director (left); Zhang Ziyi, actress

© Ports International

Portrait reflecting 21st-century value systems in China

© Pierre Xiao Lu

A dinner party at a trendy Western-style restaurant in Beijing, 2006.

*A Internet Commercial of M-Zone, a Service
of China Mobile Targeting Young People, 2007*

(Clockwise) A Chinese lady sporting a Rolex watch, relaxing at the Café de la Pais, Paris (2006); a Chinese skier in Chamonix, France (2007); a Chinese socialite dressed in Agnes B and wearing Chanel cosmetics, holidaying at Cote d'Azur, France (2007); a Chinese client being measured for an Italian suit at Ports 1961 in Beijing (2007).

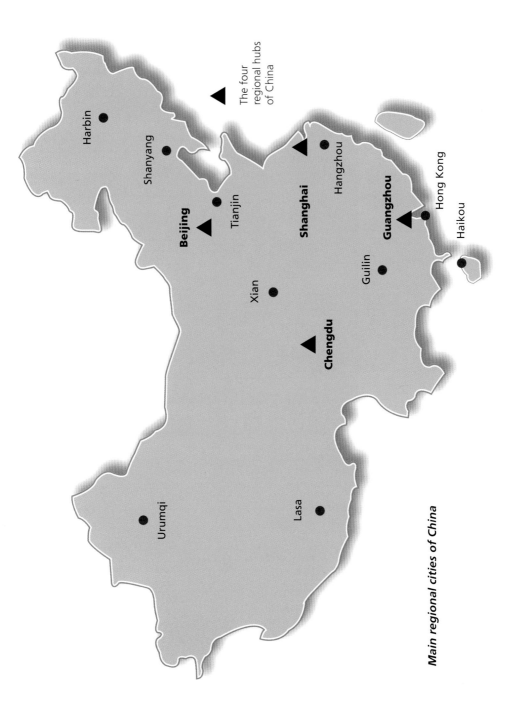

Main regional cities of China

The four
regional hubs
of China

Harbin

Shanyang

Beijing
Tianjin

Shanghai
Hangzhou

Guangzhou
Hong Kong
Haikou

Guilin

Xian

Chengdu

Urumqi

Lasa

Peninsula Palace Hotel, Beijing

© Pierre Xiao Lu

***Seasons Place with Louis Vuitton
store under construction (2007)***

© Pierre Xiao Lu

***Plaza 66, Nanjing West Road,
Shanghai***

© Pierre Xiao Lu

No. 18 and No. 3 on the Bund in Shanghai

© Pierre Xiao Lu

Kate Moss with Ports International

© Ports International

CHAPTER 1

Luxury Consumption and China's Elite

All are past and gone!

For truly great men

Look to this age alone

Mao Zedong, *Snow*

Luxury consumption and Chinese elite in ancient times

Statistics show that China has become the fourth-largest consumer for Louis Vuitton, the fifth for Gucci, the third for Mont Blanc, and the tenth for Swiss-made watches (it is, in fact, the #1 market for the Swatch Group). Without doubt, the Chinese market is one of the biggest markets for all luxury brands and has tremendous potential. In the next 10 years, affluent Chinese consumers, with their enormous purchasing power and trend-defining lifestyles, will reshape the luxury market like never before.[1]

The long history of China and its long-founded traditions give Chinese consumers the inherent ability to appreciate the beauty of luxury products and to enjoy their possession.

Chinese scholar-bureaucrats and luxury consumption

Though it may not be well-known to the Western world, luxury consumption has existed throughout China's long history. The luxury culture was highly appreciated by the Chinese upper class and has had a profound influence on Chinese society. In 1899, in his famous book *The Theory of the Leisure Class*, Thorstein Veblen[2] pointed out the conspicuous behavior of the leisure class in Western society and their social need for consuming luxury products: "The basis on which good repute in any highly organized industrial community ultimately rests is pecuniary strength; and the means of showing pecuniary strength, and so of gaining or retaining a good name, are leisure and a conspicuous consumption of goods."

In China "the leisure class" has a much longer history which can be traced back to the Spring and Autumn period and the Warring States period in the East Zhou dynasty (770–221 B.C.). During these periods, the scholar-bureaucrat class emerged as the elite class, a position it maintained for more than 2,000 years, as Max Weber explained in his second major work on the sociology of religion, *Konfuziamismus und Taoismus*. However, unlike the Brahmans in India, membership of China's scholar-bureaucrat class was neither hereditary nor exclusionist, even in early feudal society.

By the time of Emperor Han WuDi (156–87 B.C.), society was organized according to the doctrine of Confucianism and the scholar-bureaucrat class helped the emperor manage the country with the thoughts and philosophy of Confucianism. By the Sui dynasty (581–617 A.D.), China had established *Ke Ju* (科举制度), the national examination system for selecting talented young people to be scholar-bureaucrats and thus to make their contribution to the management of the country. The system allowed talented young people to change their social position through their personal efforts. This national examination system is still the main approach of the Chinese education system today in selecting young talent.

Through their educational and cultural accomplishments and the tremendous fortune and power that accompanied these, the Chinese leisure class formed a lifestyle which incorporated luxury consumption into their daily lives, in what the French refer to as "l'Art de vivre".

In imperial China, the social ranking was *shi, nong, gong, shang* (士・农・工・商): the scholar-bureaucrats, the farmers, the artisans, and, last of all, the despised merchants. Remnants of this are still present today.

It is a similar case in the Western world where, for example, the partiality of America's ruling classes toward the profession of the law has a long pedigree too (Seven of the first 10 U.S. presidents were lawyers.) In Asia, many high-level statesmen are scholars or lawyers: Lee Kuan Yew, the former prime minister of Singapore, and Dr. Han Myung-sook, the former prime minister of South Korea, are but two. In China, among the highest national leaders, almost all are technocrats who graduated from the prestigious Tsinghua University and Peking University in Beijing or Fudan University in Shanghai. Such men include President Hu Jintao and Vice-President Wu Bangguo.

The warrior spirit was also one of the most important aspects of the lifestyle of the Chinese elite. The younger members of royal and scholar-bureaucrat families were obliged to practice hunting and martial arts in order to encourage and maintain the values long associated with war and pillage which, as Veblen pointed out, brings glory and wealth. In peacetime, elegant sports such as polo, developed on the basis of hunting and martial arts, were reserved for aristocrats and were very popular in the courts of the Tang, Song, and Yuan dynasties. This elite sport combines intelligence, technique, and strength, and in the Guimet Museum in Paris there is a group of beautiful statues of young aristocrat ladies playing polo with their maids of honor.

Scholar-bureaucrats selected to help the emperor manage the country were from both the aristocracy and ordinary families. They were senior intellectuals and scholars and, in addition to the sporting activities mentioned earlier, their lifestyle incorporated fine art and aesthetics (music, calligraphy, and painting). It was a hedonistic way of life in which white spirits, gastronomy, and eroticism also figured largely.

In Bourdieu's theory,[3] taste in cultural matters is a function of educational level and social origin. The concept of "cultural capital" consists of two main factors: social origin, or a family background that is culturally refined for generations; and formal education, whereby people further develop a mastery of aesthetic codes. In consumer behavior studies, these two factors together constitute the socio-cultural environment, one of the two external influences to be considered in the input stage of the model of consumer decision-making. Together with a firm's marketing efforts, socio-cultural environment will influence the consumer's recognition of his need for certain products. Here, Bourdieu's theory is reconfirmed by the case of the Chinese scholar-bureaucrat class.

The lifestyle of the scholar-bureaucrats was a luxurious lifestyle in ancient China, one made possible by their social status, educational level, and stable income. These high-level intellectuals naturally understood the beauty of life and in their leisure time enjoyed every detail of their personal collections, which included private houses (the classical gardens of Suzhou[4]), lacquer ware, faience and porcelains, gold and jewelry, decoration and stationery (the four treasures of the study: writing brush, ink stick, ink slab and paper), furniture (a favorite category for connoisseurs of the Ming dynasty), white spirits, and gastronomy.

The pursuit of fine art and craftsmanship can be recognized in the spirit of the philosophies of the Chinese elite. Many scholar-bureaucrats, as well as emperors, were also famous poets, painters, and calligraphers. They were both the "makers" and the "clients" of Chinese fine arts. Their highly sophisticated craftsmanship enabled them to produce high-quality work and to admire those qualities in others. For example, Song Hui Zong, Zhaoji (1082–1135), a Song dynasty emperor famous for his political negotiation and compromise in the face of threats of invasion from the north, was also one of the most accomplished painters and calligraphers in the history of China. He was also a collector and connoisseur of porcelain and art and influenced the development of Chinese porcelain and notions of beauty in that period. Ming Xi Zong, Tianqi (1605–27), a Ming dynasty emperor, was a famous carpenter whose excellent technique and aesthetics contributed to the connoisseurship in the furniture of that period.

In the Western world, the production of such fine and aesthetic objects has evolved into the luxury industry. Famous craftsmen such as Hèrmes, Guerlain, and Dom Perignon created their own brands. The quest of the luxury brands is to combine tradition and modernity, craftsmanship and creativity, history and innovation. Although this has yet to be fully achieved in China because of the instability of almost 150 years of history (from the first Opium War in 1840 to the beginning of Deng's opening and reform policy in 1978), the admirable lifestyle of the ancient elite and their pursuit of the finer things in life still remain in the minds of Chinese people today. The rapidly increasing numbers of affluent Chinese consumers are not only the source of enormous purchasing power for imported luxury brands, but also serve as a reminder to Chinese luxury brands to recall the lifestyle of their ancestors from China's long and splendid past. We will discuss the opportunities open to Chinese luxury brands in later chapters.

These influences reach beyond national boundaries, and are making their way into other East Asian countries as well.

Conspicuous consumption in Confucianism-influenced countries

In recent decades, conspicuous consumption has developed rapidly in China, in Asia's Four Little Dragons (South Korea, Singapore, Taiwan, and Hong Kong) and particularly in areas strongly influenced by Chinese Confucianism. Western luxury brands have shown a very high rate of increase in these countries in recent years. For example, in the first three quarters of 2006, 18% of the Moet-Hennessy Louis-Vuitton Group's net sales came from Asia (excluding Japan).[5] Four of the five main business sectors have enjoyed double-digit revenue growth: Wines & Spirits (+24%), Fashion & Leather Goods (+20%), Perfumes & Cosmetics (+24%), and Watches & Jewelry (+18%). The fifth sector, Selective Retailing, was at +8%. Total sales also increased by 17% over the previous year.

In Veblen's theory, conspicuous behavior suggests that the rich prefer to pay high prices because this advertises the fact that they can afford such things as a necklace by Van Cleef & Arpels, while simultaneously excluding those who can't. Veblen points out that for the leisure class the price tag is essential for status. This willingness to pay more when comparable merchandise is available for much less is what economists now refer to as "the Veblen effect."

However, conspicuous consumption is not the only form of display behavior among the leisure class. In Asian countries, the socio-cultural environment also exerts a strong influence on display behaviors and is the main reason for "luxury fever" in Asia.

Confucianism and conspicuousness

The Asian social value system is based on Confucianism. The traditional eight virtues—faithfulness, filial piety, benevolence, love, courtesy, loyalty, frugality, and a sense of shame (忠孝仁爱礼义廉耻)—are the moral pillars by which society is supported. These values are an integral part of social behavior and thus manifest also in the consumer behavior of the leisure class today: "collective consciousness" and family, glory and respect, glory and awareness of shame.

Collectiveness and family are the key Confucian elements that influence Asian societies and guide individual behavior. The direct impact of this on luxury consumption is that Asian luxury consumers focus more on brands than on the products themselves. The more famous the brand, the more Asian consumers will buy and the more recognition they get from the public. This is one of the major reasons for the success of the ostentatious luxury brands such as Rolex, Louis Vuitton, Armani, Gucci, and Christian Dior in Asian countries.

Respect and superiority: Asian people influenced by Confucianism believe that one of the fundamental needs is to be respected by others. Having this respect is a key indicator of social superiority. This respect can be gained and expressed in every aspect of daily life. To acquire the respect of others, people in ancient time made efforts to be selected as scholar-bureaucrats through a series of state-organized examinations. In today's society, the need of respect is expressed in different ways, with conspicuous consumption being the easiest and fastest way to attract others' attention. While having a Ferrari or a Porsche is a clear display of the owner's wealth, owning a Rolls Royce or a Bentley not only displays wealth, but also indicates power and social status. The intrinsic value of the luxury products they consume and the awareness of the luxury brand among the public can fulfill people's need to impress others and establish superiority.

Glory and awareness of shame is another element which pressures people to succeed in society. An individual should bring glory and respect to the family and to the wider community, and displaying the visible symbols of success is one way of doing this. Wearing luxury brands can be a direct and clear sign to society that says, "I am someone successful and respected." The consequence is that wearing a luxury brand can help deflect any suspicion of shame in a family-oriented society, regardless of whether the individual is actually successful or not. It can even lead to them being classified among the elite without any personal effort or family heritage. Thus, this kind of pressure often pushes people toward vanity and the need to hide the true reality. The reason why some Asian women are crazy about Louis Vuitton bags is not simply because of the trendy design and the French origin of the brand. There are surely more profound social explanations.

Demography of consumer generations and social classes

Some form of class structure or social rank has existed in all societies throughout human history.[6] Different social classes have widely differing values, attitudes, and behaviors. Social scientists associate these classes with specific demographic and other categorical data in an effort to determine if certain groups can be said to possess specific orientations (attitudes), which may explain some of their behaviors.[7]

In Western society, the social classes are classified into the following six groups: upper-upper class, lower-upper class, upper-middle class, lower-middle class, upper-lower class, and, finally, lower-lower class. The leisure class in Veblen's theory is a hybrid concept of two or more classes.

The leisure class has a strong correlation with conspicuous consumption because of the socio-economic status of its members. The lower-upper class (new wealth) and the upper-middle class (achieving professionals) are more conspicuous in their consumption (see Table 1.2) than the upper-upper class (country-club establishment). Luxury brands and goods largely fulfill the demands of conspicuous consumption because of their special product attributes and significations, such as higher price, aesthetics, excellent quality, and so on. Therefore, the lower-upper class and the upper-middle class are the major targets for luxury goods because of their economic bases (income) and social recognition demands (social and cultural factors).[8]

Dr. Yuwa Hedrick-Wong's recent research[9] into affluent consumers in Asia identifies two segments: the "mass affluent" and the "rich." The income definitions of these two segments are summarized in Table 1.1.

TABLE 1.1: *Income definitions (in US$)*

Market	Income Level of Mass Affluent Households	Income Level of Rich Households
Australia	$100,000–$250,000	$250,000+
China	$7,500–$50,000	$50,000+
Hong Kong	$100,000–$250,000	$250,000+
India	$7,500–$50,000	$50,000+
Japan	$100,000–$250,000	$250,000+
Korea	$75,000–$200,000	$200,000+
Malaysia	$30,000–$100,000	$100,000+
Philippines	$15,000–$75,000	$75,000+
Singapore	$100,000–$250,000	$250,000+
Taiwan	$75,000–$200,000	$200,000+
Thailand	$30,000–$100,000	$100,000+

The income criteria for the "mass affluent" and the "rich" vary from country to country, because the effects of "purchasing power parity" (PPP) is also taken into account. This means that in different markets an equivalent unit of money could have very different purchasing power. Thus, the income thresholds for affluent and rich households are generally lower in lower-income countries or regions. For example, in Australia, mass-affluent households are defined as those who earn between US$100,000 and US$250,000 per year, and rich households are those who earn above US$250,000. Japan, Hong Kong, and Singapore share the same criteria.

However, in China and India, the income thresholds are much lower, at US$7,500 to US$50,000 for mass-affluent households and more than US$50,000 a year for rich households.

The mass affluent and the rich in the different markets share common underlying characteristics as consumers, which forms the basis of the cross-market comparison.

Emerging upper-middle class and super-rich: The Chinese elite

In today's Chinese society, social class distribution is changing with the economic evolution. A new social class has been emerging in economically developed urban areas (Beijing, Shanghai, Guangzhou, Shenzhen, Chengdu, Chongqing, and so on) which have benefited from the opening economic policy since 1979. The social class distribution is not completely developed. The majority (about one billion) of the Chinese population still live in rural areas. Consequently, Chinese social classes have not been as clearly differentiated as those described in American society (Table 1.2).

However, because of their socio-economic status some people in China hold favorable social positions similar to Veblen's "leisure class." These approximate to the lower-upper and upper-middle class definition in Table 1.2 and "the mass affluent" and "the rich" in Dr. Hedrick-Wong's research. This section of society is the Chinese elite and they are the core clients of luxury brands.

These are the opinion leaders in Chinese society, despite the fact that the majority live in the countryside. The opinions of these well-educated elite influence lifestyle trends, attitudes of the media, and interests of business. Their professional achievements and private lifestyles lead the evolution of the Chinese consumer society; they are the models of success to be imitated by the people in the mass market who aspire to join them.

TABLE 1.2: *Social-class profiles[10] and the equivalent in China*

CHINA'S SUPER RICH, *but not yet with historical heritage*

The Upper-Upper Class: *Country-Club Establishment*
- Small number of well-established families
- Belong to best country clubs and sponsor major charity events
- Serve as trustees for local colleges and hospitals
- Prominent physicians and lawyers
- May be heads of major financial institutions, owners of major long-established firms
- Accustomed to wealth, so do not spend money conspicuously

CHINA ELITE

The Lower-Upper Class: *New Wealth*
- Not quite accepted by the upper crust of society
- Represent "new money"
- Successful business executives
- Conspicuous users of their new wealth

The Upper-Middle Class: *Achieving Professionals*
- Have neither family status nor unusual wealth
- Career-oriented
- Young successful professionals, corporate managers, and business owners
- Most are college graduates, many with advanced degrees
- Active in professional, community, and social activities
- Have a keen interest in obtaining the "better things in life"
- Their homes serve as symbols of their achievements
- Very child-oriented
- Consumption is often conspicuous

WORKING CLASS

The Lower-Middle Class: *Faithful Followers*
- Primarily non-managerial white-collar workers and highly paid blue-collar workers
- Want to achieve "respectability" and be accepted as good citizens
- Want their children to be well-behaved
- Tend to be churchgoers and are often involved in church-sponsored activities
- Prefer a neat and clean appearance and tend to avoid faddish or highly-stylish clothing
- Constitute a major market for do-it-yourself products

A luxury brand should always focus on the elite and the leisure class of a society rather than on the mass market. It should define new trends in fashion and luxury, thus attracting the attention of the opinion leaders and luxury clients.

Social class is defined by the socio-economic variables of family income, occupational status, and educational attainment. In previous studies of Chinese urban consumers, four basic social classes were defined by demographic criteria: working poor, salary class, little rich, and yuppies.[11] Other research has defined the Chinese elite according to the following criteria: business profile (for example, CEO or senior manager), company operations (for example, China only or international), and personal profile (average age, university education, and average monthly personal income).

Thus, "Chinese elite" is not simply a demographic and economic term; it is also a social-class term. From a demographic point of view, the majority of the Chinese elite are under 45 years old. In fact, the average age of the 100 richest mainland Chinese is 45 years; the youngest is only 25.[12] China's historical background made it impossible for such a social category to emerge before 1978. From 1949, all China's old wealth was appropriated by the state through a series of measures to nationalize private business, a process which saw the complete disappearance of the private sector by the mid-1950s. The last vestiges of the old-wealth heritage of lifestyle and thinking were removed by the Cultural Revolution (1966–76). It was only with the re-establishment of the higher education system in 1978 that 18-year-olds were able to acquire the basic cultural assets that would enable them to be classified as elite in the future. By 2006, such individuals would be no more than 45 or 46 years old.

Since the founding of the People's Republic of China in 1949, there have been five generations of consumers, with clearly different lifestyles and visions of the world: the New China generation, the Lost generation, the Suffering generation, the Transitional generation, and the One-child generation.

The New China generation

Born before 1945, they are eyewitnesses to the momentous changes of 1949 and are the builders of the new communist China. Most of them had a good education before the start of the Cultural Revolution in 1966, held important positions in society, and are currently approaching retirement. Hu Jintao, the president, and Wen Jiabao, the premier of China, are good examples of this generation, most of whom are the parents of the Transitional generation.

The Lost generation

Born between 1945 and 1960 (about 225 million people), they grew up with political instability: the Great Leap Forward (in the late 1950s) and the Cultural Revolution (1966–76), as well as three years of natural disasters (in the early 1960s). They had no chance to receive formal education during their adolescence, being obliged to return to the countryside to work alongside the peasants for a very long period. When they returned to the cities, their lack of skills and training meant that they could do only basic manual work in factories. However, most of the state-owned factories were inefficient and were closed during the economic reforms that began in 1978, leaving many unemployed and unemployable.

As victims of the social upheavals that followed 1949, they had to seek social recognition in other ways: hard work, connections, and so on. Once their economic situation began to change for the better, enabling them to enjoy a more affluent lifestyle, their desire for social recognition manifested itself in overt displays of showing-off.

Since they couldn't reclaim their lost youth, they transferred their hopes and ideals to their children, investing a great deal of money, energy, and time in their offspring. The introduction of the one-child policy in the early 1980s complicated matters for a typical Chinese family and left a big gap in Chinese society—a gap that had to be filled by the next generation.

The Suffering generation

Born between 1960 and 1970 (about 300 million people), they grew up during the Cultural Revolution. Some became the first university students after 1978 and the social pillars of today's China. They witnessed the instability of the Cultural Revolution and then experienced the new climate ushered in with Deng's opening and reform policy in 1978, which enabled them to give full rein to their creativity and ideals. On the one hand, they were still conservative, hard-working people, the carriers of traditional Chinese values; on the other, they were the first generation to see the world through an opened window and eager to know the new things outside China. They had hopes for their country; that it would become strong and efficient, delivering to its people a free and happy life. This generation also witnessed the events of Tiananmen Square in 1989. Experiencing the struggle between their pursuit of liberty and democracy on one side, and the traditional values and communist system on the other, they were able to think more about the future of China than the Lost generation.

Some seized the opportunities open to them, created their own companies and went on to become the earliest of the current Chinese elite. They achieved their success through pioneering pathways, professional achievement, and inheritance. Many famous artists, novelists, actors, and film directors are numbered among this generation, including Yu Hua, the novelist, Gong Li, the actress, and Jiang Wen, the actor and film director.

The Transitional generation

Born between 1970 and 1979 (about 205 million people), this generation grew up in the era of reform and opening up that resulted in the rapid development of the national economy away from centralized planning to a market system. Growing up in an environment that offers more stability and greater opportunities, they are more optimistic, active, and dynamic than their parents' generation and have the confidence to re-conquer the world.

While the Transitional generation inherited the value systems of the previous generation, it has embraced the new and resolved the conflicts between them. Zhang Ziyi, the actress, and Xu Jinglei, the film director, are typical of this generation.

The One-child generation

Born between 1979 and 1990 (about 227 million people) into a relatively affluent environment, all are products of the one-child policy and thus have grown up receiving much more care and attention from their parents and grandparents. As the children of the Lost generation, they are protected and doted upon.

They have grown up in an era with little social instability and in which education is seen as the key to social standing. This is reflected in their thoughts and behavior. They are more confident, self-conscious, self-centered, open to new trends, weary of traditional moral doctrines, sensitive to criticism, and with a tendency to avoid unpleasant realities. They are more oriented to materialism and hedonism.

After the One-child generation, will be the E generation, born after 1990. They live in the age of information technology and the Internet revolution and are too young yet to be considered as part of the elite. But their time will come.

The current Chinese elite are drawn mainly from the Suffering generation and the Transitional generation, with the One-Child generation about to enter the picture.

From a socio-economic viewpoint, the annual family income of the Chinese elite is considered to be at least 10 times the national average income in any given year.[13] Currently, the annual elite income is a minimum of RMB120,000 (equivalent to US$15,000). This bottom line is higher than the threshold for "mass affluent" consumers set out in previous research. An international criterion for membership of the middle class is US$6,000 per capita per year (RMB5,000 per capita per month).[14] In China the middle-class annual family income standard is from US$7,264 to US$60,532 (from RMB60,000 to RMB500,000) per year per family.[15] With an average position in a dynamic business, individuals can earn more than the baseline of $15,000 per year, which is enough to ensure that they can easily afford luxury products and services. Such cases are very different from, say, those that often appear in the media highlighting young girls who save up to two or three months' salary to buy a Louis Vuitton handbag in order to give the impression that they come from a wealthy family or have a rich boyfriend. Such people are more likely to be from the lower-middle class described in Table 1.2.

In addition to income level, the Chinese elite are distinguishable also by the assets they own: a comfortable residence in the suburbs or a condo in the central business district (many own two or more pieces of real estate). They are very familiar with the various financial services—insurance, bonds, funds, stocks, and so on—available for personal or family investments. Cars are indispensable.

In addition to hard work, they know how to enjoy themselves, with sports, leisure, and travel ensuring a balanced life. Constraints on their leisure time mean that many have membership in top sports clubs near to their offices or homes. Beauty and health care are also important to them, as is regular overseas travel.

The key to membership of the Chinese elite is education. A university-level education is fundamental and many, in fact, have had overseas experience, either for education or company training. With their position comes social responsibility. Their opinions and behavior form the voice of the time and influence the authorities and the majority of the people in the country. It is their education and the way they behave and exercise their responsibilities which distinguishes the elite from those who simply earn lots of money. The media often confuse these two categories: the elite and the "vulgar rich." People are often impressed by the show-off and extravagant behavior of the latter, who are simply trying to acquire the social respect which is normally given only to the elite class. One of the objectives of this book is to clarify such distinctions and to capture the essentials for understanding China's elite and their luxury consumption. Table 1.3 summarizes the specific criteria for membership of the Chinese elite.

TABLE 1.3: *Demographic and socio-economic criteria to define Chinese elite*

Demographic Criteria	Chinese Elite
Age	25–45 years old
Gender	Male and Female
Region/Cities	Beijing, Shanghai, Guangzhou, Shenzhen, Chengdu, Hangzhou, Dalian, Xi'an ... (the economic hubs)
Socio-economic Criteria	
Income	Average personal income: at least 10 times the national average
Occupational Status	Entrepreneurs, senior managers, and successful professionals etc.
Education	Bachelor's degree as a minimum (most have Master's degrees)

The Chinese elite can be considered as being equivalent to the upper-middle class and super-rich in Western society, and their numbers are increasing every year. China's national GDP growth rate is currently around 9%, but is much higher in the economic hubs and big cities such as Beijing and Shanghai where the elite are concentrated. They are the group who benefit the most from rapid economic development because of their higher level education and their key professional positions in business. In 2005, the Chinese Academy of Social Sciences estimated that there were 10,000 entrepreneurs with net assets of over US$10 million each, and some 300,000 with an individual net wealth exceeding US$1 million.

There are about five million rich (annual income RMB1 million/US$150,000+), 40 million affluent (RMB500,000/US$70,000+), and 150 million middle class (RMB100,000/US$14,000+). In total, China currently has 195 million people who can afford luxury goods and are thus potential clients for luxury brands. Among these, about 50 million qualify as elite consumers, using the criteria outlined above.

In Chapter 3, we will analyze China's value systems in the 21st century. This is the key to opening the door to understanding the behavior of the elite's attitudes toward luxury brands and luxury consumption. Before that, however, we need to clarify the confusion surrounding the concept of "luxury" and "luxury products."

ENDNOTES

1   Hedrick-Wong, Yuwa, 2007, *Succeeding Like Success: The Affluent Consumers of Asia*, John Wiley & Sons (Asia) Pte., Ltd.

2   Veblen, T., 1899, *The Theory of The Leisure Class*, Penguin Books.

3   Bourdieu, P., 1979, *La Distinction, Critique Sociale du Jugement*, Les Editions de Minuit.

4   The Classical Gardens of Suzhou were built during the Ming and Qing dynasties (16th–18th centuries), and were listed as World Heritage in 1997.

5   LVMH Group 2006, *Third Quarter Revenue Report*.

6   Schiffman and Kanuk, 2000, *Consumer Behavior*, Seventh Edition, p.306, Prentice Hall.

7   Konty and Dunham, 1997, "Differences in Value and Attitude Change Over the Life Course", *Sociological Spectrum* 17:177–97.

8   Dubois, Bernard and Duquesne, Patrick, 1993, "The Market for Luxury Goods: Income versus Culture", *European Journal of Marketing*, Vol. 27, No.1, pp.35–44.

9   Hedrick-Wong, op. cit.

10 Schiffman and Kanuk, op. cit.

11 Cui, Geng and Liu, Qiming, 2001, "Executive Insights: Emerging Market Segments in a Transitional Economy: A study of Urban Consumers in China", *Journal of International Marketing*.

12 Hurun Report 2006, www.hurun.net: Hu run, a former journalist for *Forbes* in China, publishes an annual, independent, report listing China's 100 richest people.

13 For example, according to the State Statistical Bureau in 1998, the average annual household income in China was RMB16,549; in 2003, the national GDP was around US$1,000 per capita.

14 United Nations Human Development Report (HDR) 2004, "Millennium Development Goals: A compact among nations to end human poverty".

15 Annual Report of National Statistics Bureau, Beijing, 2005.

CHAPTER 2

The Confused Concept of "Luxury"

No Impetuosity, No Arrogance, No Showing off.

Lu Kun (1536–1618, Ming dynasty), *Shen Yin Yu*

I N TODAY'S CHINA, the concept of luxury is confused, partially because of the inappropriate Chinese translation of the word "luxury" and the negative connotations of extravagance in Chinese history and culture. However, in the Western world, "luxury" and "extravagance" have different connotations. It is in this context that we will discuss why the concept of luxury in today's China is confused.

The concept of luxury in Western cultures

A number of Western economists and sociologists—amongst them, Mauss, Veblen, Battle, Elias, and Bourdieu—have viewed luxury as a symbolic show, a demonstration of social distinction and class. However, as discussed by Lipovetsky and Roux,[1] in the past two decades the concept of luxury has taken a post-modernist turn, which sees luxury as being in the process of deinstitutionalization, since it is derived from the concept of family, sexuality, and religion. In the culture of post-individualism, luxury is emotional, experimental, and psychological. For the moral critic, the concept of luxury is the proud expression of an insatiable desire to overcome the harshness of a complex existence. On the other hand, there is the social critic, for whom luxury is the conspicuous sign of people's fight to improve their social position, their aspirations to belong to a higher class.

Against a backdrop of post-modernism in European and North American societies, luxury brands also changed their business logic from family hand-crafted traditions to a more market-oriented perspective. The conglomerates such as LVMH, Richemont, and PPR-Gucci restructured the independent and family-owned luxury brands into powerful luxury giants, as the market expanded to incorporate the middles classes. The concept of luxury has become more "democratized" in Western cultures.

Other researchers have defined luxury in different ways. Danielle Allérès[2] distinguishes three different levels of luxury: inaccessible—exclusive models and unique hand-made pieces; intermediary—expensive replicas of individual models; and accessible—all products made in bulk in factories or workshops. For her, the majority of luxury business today falls into this last category, echoing the theme of democratization.

Michel Chevalier and Gérald Mazzalovo[3] have proposed that a true luxury brand has a strong artistic content, craftsmanship, and an international appeal that differentiates it from common products. The luxury product— the work of talented designers and sophisticated craftsmen— is an object with beauty and has an emotional content that lends itself to being given as a gift to commemorate significant moments in people's lives. It will have an almost-global presence, being available in all of the world's great cities.

The meaning of luxury products in Asian countries

Gutman's means-end chain theory[4] suggested that products seek to tie the consumption of such products to the satisfaction of desired values. For luxury goods, the semiotic and symbolic characteristics of the product and of the brand are highly significant and often become the symbol which attracts the consumers.

In a recent study of the Chinese elite's attitude toward luxury goods,[5] six attributes were identified as the criteria for luxury products: excellent quality, very high price, scarcity/uniqueness, aesthetic and emotional content, brand history and heritage, and the fact that they are basically inessential/superfluous. In addition, some other aspects of luxury which are especially relevant in the Asian cultural context should also be taken into account—conspicuousness, display, and "dream value."[6]

Excellent quality

This is the essence of a luxury product, which guarantees reliability and durability. According to Dubois et al.,[7] there are two major indicators of quality here: the first refers to the perceived exceptional nature of the ingredients or components used, such as the big stones on Cartier rings. The second is based on the perceived delicacy and expertise involved in manufacturing products or delivering services, such as that used by Hermès, which applies the same traditional craftsmanship to produce modern handbags and Swiss watches as it did to craft saddles and fine equestrian equipment.

These are the inherent values sought by China's true luxury consumers, who are more concerned with the beauty and intricacies offered by Breguet or Patek Philippe than by more ostentatious displays of wealth. These are in the minority, however, because, as we saw in the previous chapter, the general perception of the Chinese luxury consumer is one of overt, conspicuous consumption, where the focus is on the more flashy, social aspects

Very high price

A very high price is considered to be a logical consequence of perceived excellence in quality. The Veblen effect—the higher the price is, the more the rich buy—is illustrated at every luxury goods and auto show in China: all the most expensive models of Rolls-Royce are sold out on the first day.

Scarcity and uniqueness

These characteristics, too, are closely associated with perceived quality and high prices. Scarcity is not limited to the nature of the offering
but also extends to its availability and usage. You may have to wait for
months for a Hermès Kelly or Birkin bag; and for certain brands of Swiss
watches the wait may be measured in years rather than months. The "limited collection" concept is one often employed by luxury fashion brands:
Lacoste's "techno-polo" and "eco-polo" were launched in order to create
the uniqueness of the special model.

Chinese luxury consumers are starting to discover the scarcity and
uniqueness aspect of luxury goods. In general, they are not patient and
don't believe in joining a queue outside a store to get what they want.
The belief is that if they can afford it, they should be able to buy it
immediately. But this doesn't always prove to be the case and they are
having to learn that spending money is also a fine art, and patience is
part of the game.

Aesthetic and emotional content

At this level, luxury products become pieces of art. This attribute is
expected from the goods themselves because of the context in which they
are presented as well as the perception of the people who consume these
goods. The aesthetic and emotional content creates a sentimental attachment to the luxury brands from their consumers. From ancient times,
the Chinese have shown an appreciation of fine arts and have managed
to integrate the aesthetic into their daily lives, as we saw in the previous
chapter. There is a strong demand from, and a need within, the Chinese
market for real Chinese luxury brands which reflect this. However, Chinese brands have yet to attain the sophistication of a luxury brand and
Western brands are too remote from the traditional Chinese way of fine
living, leaving something of a vacuum.

Brand history and heritage

A long history and tradition are demanded of luxury products and services, adding a twist to the famous "time is money" adage. The history and heritage of the luxury houses is something than cannot be copied by new entrants to the market and this is what gives the long-standing French and Italian luxury brands an important competitive advantage. A new luxury brand needs time to write its own history, to build a heritage. Their task is to get consumers to pay premium prices to share in that process.

Chinese luxury consumers are extremely interested in the history and the legends of the luxury firms, opening a door for international brands to introduce new concepts of products and services, and to make direct contact with local consumers, to involve them in the histories and legends of the founders and designers of fashion dynasties. In this way, Chinese consumers will become very familiar with the brands and associate their personal experiences with those of the luxury brands, creating an ideal opportunity for foreign brands to build local legitimacy and loyalty among local consumers.

Inessential/superfluous

Luxury products are not, in themselves, necessary for survival. The diamonds around the face of a Rolex, for example, do not help it work any more precisely than a plastic Casio digital watch. Certainly the Rolex fulfills its function as a watch—to indicate time—but it also serves to reflect the wealth and social status of its wearer. In the emerging new wealth of today's China, this role of luxury business as a social indicator will continue to dominate market trends for a long time to come.

Dream value

This is an important element for Asian luxury consumers. A luxury product has the capacity to make consumers dream of possessing it, whatever the nature of their attachment to it. They aspire to become part of what luxury products represent and, as soon as their finances permit, are very happy to fulfill long-held dreams by buying goods and brands that help them satisfy their personal and social aspirations.

Conspicuousness

Following the first industrial revolution in Europe in the 18th century, a new social class—the leisure class—emerged and introduced a bourgeois lifestyle. Conspicuous behavior became necessary for the *nouveau riche* to show off their wealth and demand respect from noble families and common people alike. As Veblen's analysis has shown, the emergence of a leisure class and their conspicuous behavior are inevitable expressions of social and economic evolution.

As we saw in Chapter 1, China has a long history, and the desire for well-designed, high-quality products was as clear in the Chinese royal court as it was in any of the courts of Europe. The exchange of gifts between countries (in fact, between two royal courts) existed over several centuries. However, Columbus's discovery of the New World, colonialism, and two world wars all served to drive Asian countries into political and economic turmoil, with damaging effects for their traditional luxury industries and artisans' workshops. This is one of the reasons why there are few traditional luxury brands in Asian countries, especially in China.

"Learning from Westerners" became common for Asian countries after reflecting on their own experiences of social evolution and their contacts with the West. The first mover was Japan, which launched its Meiji Modernization at the end of the 19th century. After the Second World War, and with the presence of American forces in some Asian regions, industrialization brought economic development and wealth. Western lifestyles became *à la mode* for the elite and for the young; consuming Western luxury products became a symbol of success and an indicator of financial strength.

In Chinese-dominated societies such as Hong Kong, Taiwan, and Singapore, the majority of people are descendants of war refugees, poor farmers, and fishermen who fled poverty in their native country to earn a living elsewhere during times of hardship and war. Their financial situations improved and they went on to become the "new rich" of Asia. They then behaved in much the same way as their 18th- and 19th-century European and American counterparts: that is to say, in need of social recognition and respect, they engaged in the kind of conspicuous consumption that met their social and psychological needs.

In Mainland China, after 30 years of an opening and flexible economic policy, the country is entering into the same period of transition. Once again, conspicuous consumption is becoming a hallmark of the "new rich" class. However, what is different this time is that this class is no longer counted by tens of thousands, but by millions or tens of millions.

The connotations of luxury (奢侈 *shē chǐ*) and its negative impacts on luxury consumption

The concept and definition of the word "luxury" is not the same in Chinese as it is in Latin languages. The Chinese translated word is literal and cannot cover the full significance of the English word. The connotations in Chinese are quite different from the original meaning of luxury in Western culture.

The word "luxury" can be used both as a noun and as an adjective. Both capture the comfort entailed in the regular use and enjoyment of the finest in food and drink, clothes, and surroundings. It connotes the enjoyment of expensive, though inessential, items such as caviar and champagne. Though there is an undoubted element of indulgence involved, the word is essentially neutral in tone, free of criticism, actual or implied.

The word "luxury" is translated in Chinese as the word "奢侈", "*shē chǐ*". It consists of two characters: "奢" (*shē*), meaning "extravagant"[8] and "侈" (*chǐ*), meaning "arrogant and wasteful".[9] Together, the characters combine to form a word that indicates dissipation and the wasteful use of wealth; the over-pursuit of enjoyment. The term has clear pejorative overtones.

But, apart from the sense of enjoyment that each carries, the words "luxury" and "*shē chǐ*" have little in common and I do not believe that this is an appropriate translation.

The first translation of a Latin language into Chinese was conducted by Catholic missionaries and Chinese scholar-bureaucrats during the Qing dynasty (1644–1911). The translation was not exactly precise because the word "*shē chǐ*" had been in existence for a very long time before this and was widely used to describe the extravagant behavior of the rich. This translation was adopted and continues today, creating great confusion for the luxury business in China.

The negative connotation is thus carried over into terms such as luxury product (奢侈品 *shē chǐ pin*), luxury industry (奢侈品行业 *shē chǐ pin hang ye*), luxury goods (奢侈货品, *shē chǐ huo pin*), luxury business (奢侈品商业 *shē chǐ pin shang ye*), and so on.

The problem is that throughout China's long history, the social morals and doctrines of Confucianism, Taoism, and Buddhism have taught that life should have no impetuosity, no arrogance, and no showing off. Frugality, the antonym of "*shē chǐ*," is considered to be one of the Chinese virtues and encouraged both by the emperors in ancient China and the current communist government. Thus when the idea of a luxury product carries with it connotations of extravagance and wastefulness, this is likely to give rise to psychological conflicts in potential buyers.

On top of these traditional cultural values mobilizing its national machinery and the huge network of party members, the Chinese government has recently set about propagating a value system for China in the 21st century. Based on socialist concepts of honor and disgrace, the objective is to maintain and enforce the leading position of the Chinese Communist Party in society.

Honor and disgrace

In most studies of Chinese consumers, researchers have ignored one of the most powerful influences on today's Chinese society—the propaganda of the Chinese Communist Party and the central government. They forget that China is a socialist country in which the guiding principle is "socialism with Chinese characteristics": a philosophy that is perhaps at odds with that of the luxury industry.

One of the fundamental tenets of consumer research is to gain a deep insight into the value systems of the target market, in order to better understand social trends, lifestyles, and consumer needs. Having this information, designers and managers working in the luxury industry can then find ways of bringing the values of their particular brand and products to that particular market.

In recent communications in the media the Chinese government has, for the first time, launched a campaign to build a value system based on the notions of honor and disgrace. This threatens to have a major impact on the luxury industry, since government officials are amongst the biggest consumers of certain luxury products and brands. For example, Ermenegildo Zegna is one of the most successful fashion brands in China, being the brand of choice for senior government officials. Very quickly, Zegna became a symbol of power, and middle and lower-rank officials began to imitate their superiors. Given that China has some 10.6 million government officials, the potential market for fashion brands is huge.

In 2005, President Hu Jintao introduced the "socialist concept of honor and disgrace" (社会主义荣辱观), advocating "modern socialist virtues." At the Tenth National Committee of the Chinese People's Political Consultative Conference (CPPCC)—China's political advisory body—Hu stressed the importance of developing an "advanced socialist culture."

The concept, which is designed to refresh China's values by amalgamating traditional values with modern virtues, is set out in Table 2.1.

TABLE 2.1: *Socialist concept of honor and disgrace — Eight Dos and Don'ts (Eight Honors & Eight Disgraces, 八荣八耻)*

1. Love, don't harm, the motherland
   （以热爱祖国为荣、以危害祖国为耻）
2. Serve, don't deviate from, the people
   （以服务人民为荣、以背离人民为耻）
3. Believe in science; don't be ignorant and unenlightened
   （以崇尚科学为荣、以愚昧无知为耻 ）
4. Work hard; don't be lazy or hate work
   （以辛勤劳动为荣、以好逸恶劳为耻）
5. Be united and help each other; don't gain benefits at the expense
   of others （以团结互助为荣、以损人利己为耻）
6. Be honest and trustworthy; do not make profit at the expense of
   your values （以诚实守信为荣、以见利忘义为耻）
7. Be disciplined and law-abiding, rather than chaotic and lawless
   （以遵纪守法为荣、以违法乱纪为耻）
8. Know plain living and hard struggle; don't indulge in luxuries and
   pleasures （以艰苦奋斗为荣、以骄奢淫逸为耻）

The point to note in the last of these is that, once again, luxury is linked with extravagance, arrogance, and waste, reinforcing the potential problems facing the luxury brands as they seek to communicate their values in China.

There are two general solutions for this. The first is to change the Chinese translation of the word for luxury from "*shē chǐ*" to "*jing pin*" (精品，high-end fine product). For example, the official translation of the Comité Colbert, the French Association of Luxury Brands, has been changed from 科尔贝华贵协会 (Colbert Luxury Association) to 法国精品协会 (French High-end Fine Products Association) to avoid potential communication problems in the Chinese media and to give Chinese clients and government a positive image without conflicting with official policy.

The second solution is to continue the use of "*shē chĭ*" as a translation for "luxury" but to confine its usage to fashion and consumer-related magazines, over which the government has less control and which do not fall directly within the political sphere.

To find coherence with official policy is an intelligent way to avoid unnecessary conflict. The reality is that China is a socialist country and the role of multinational luxury brands is to do business in China, not to change the system or the regime. Working within the system can bring unbelievable opportunities and rewards, as Audi (like Zegna) has found.

It is a rule that the limousines used by Chinese officials have to be made in China. Some 10 years ago, Audi began to manufacture the A6, a high-end model for the Chinese market. It was the only available choice and the black A6 became the official government vehicle and was thus associated with power. It is this association with power that explains why in the streets of Beijing today there are many more Audis than other up-market brands, such as Mercedes-Benz or BMW. The A6 has become the symbol of official power and influence, and owning one is a statement of status.

ENDNOTES

1   Gilles Lipovetsky and Elyette Roux, 2005, *Le Luxe éternel:De l'âge du sacré au temps des marques*, Gallimard.

2   Danielle Allérès, 1990, *Luxe, Strategie, Marketing*, Economica.

3   Michel Chevalier and Gérald Mazzalovo, 2007, *Luxury Brand Management*, John Wiley and Sons.

4   J. Gutman, 1992, "A means-end chain model based on consumer categorization processes", *Journal of Marketing* 46 (1), pp.60–72.

5   Dubois, Laurent and Czellar, 2000, "Consumer Rapport to Luxury: Analyzing Complex and Ambivalent Attitudes", working paper, HEC; Pierre Xiao Lu, 2007, "Six Characteristics of Luxury Products", *Harvard Business Review China*.

6   Dubois and Duquesne, 1993, "The Market for Luxury Goods: Income versus Culture", *European Journal of Marketing*; Lipovetsky and Roux, op. cit.; Nyeck and Roux, 2004, "Valeurs culturelles et attitudes par rapport au luxe: l'exemple du Québec", Asac Proceedings, June 13–17.

7   Dubois, et al., op. cit.

8   The original meaning of "*shē*" in old Chinese is given in *Shuowen Jiezi* by the Han dynasty writer Xu Shen as (" 奢, 张也。——《说文》。徐灏曰: " 奢者侈靡放纵之义。故曰 '张'，言其张大也。"), "extravagant", "overindulgent".

9   In *Shuowen Jiezi* the original meaning of "*chi*" ("本义:自高自大,盛气凌人; 侈,掩胁也。——《说文》。段注: "掩者,掩盖其上;胁者,胁制其旁。凡自多以陵人曰侈。此侈之本义也。") was "lift up one's horn" and conveys arrogance.

CHAPTER 3

Consumer Value Systems in 21st-Century China

The trends of the world are vast and mighty:

The ones following them will flourish,

The ones going against them will perish.

Dr. Sun Yat-sen (1866–1925)

T O **UNDERSTAND** the consumption behavior of Chinese luxury consumers, first we should examine the value systems of China in the 21st century. The attitudes and behaviors of China's elite are based on value systems which are new and quite different from the traditional value systems. Before looking at these new systems in detail, it is perhaps necessary to review some of the underlying theories anchoring the discussion.

Luxury attitudes studies

Although the paradoxical nature of luxury consumption was pointed out more than 2,000 years ago by Greek and Chinese philosophers (Aristotle, Statius, and Confucius), systematic and consumer-based studies of luxury have been relatively scarce and underdeveloped.

Market-segmentation research has shown that consumer attitudes are complicated and that three attitude types—Elitism, Democratization, and Distance—toward luxury products exist.[1] These types were identified through a 20-country survey, democratization being stronger in American or Scandinavian countries, and elitism or distance prominent in European Catholic cultures. Some communities, such as the French-speaking Canadian region, have an intermediate position.[2]

However, some limits in the existing research should be mentioned. First, this research, based on in-depth interviews and surveys, did not take into account the consumers' social categories and age differences in the quantitative analysis stage; only students were invited to take part. Demographic variables (age, gender, and region etc.) and personal background (income, education, and profession) were not considered to be relevant in shaping a consumer's attitude toward luxury in such studies. These demographic variables are considered to be minor complementary characteristics to further segment the luxury market.

Second, the attitudinal ambivalence observed and analyzed in the Dubois and Laurent study mixes social and individual dimensions. There is no discussion or debate about the differences or common points between these two dimensions of ambivalence. No distinctions are proposed.

Lastly, the third limit concerns the research samples. In the Dubois et al. study, the in-depth interviews were all conducted with French consumers. For the international survey in the second stage, the respondents who represented Asia were all from Hong Kong and it is of dubious value to generalize the conclusions drawn as being applicable to other East Asian consumers and, particularly, to Chinese luxury consumers.

East Asian luxury attitude studies

In their study of East Asian luxury consumer behavior, Wong and Ahuvia[3] proposed five aspects of Chinese traditional values that remain vital despite modernization: (1) interdependent self-concept, (2) the balance between individual and group needs, (3) hierarchy, (4) the legitimacy of group affiliations, and (5) humility. Their model, based on these five aspects, has not been empirically tested. They also fail to take into account the relations between these traditional values and the new Chinese values concerning modernization. The modern values, in the authors' eyes, are not dominant in today's Chinese society and thus are not really discussed in their study.

However, several cultural value studies[4] have shown that apparently contradictory cultural values coexist in Mainland China. For instance, in Cheng and Schweitzer's study of Chinese television commercials (1996), the authors found that "modernity," "family," and "tradition" are the three most dominant values displayed. They concluded that the Chinese value system was a melting pot of Chinese traditional values and Western values. But the question is: Do ambivalent attitudes coexist within Chinese society as a whole or are they manifest in each individual?

The conclusion drawn by Cheng and Schweitzer makes sense for the evolution of Chinese society, but the contradictory values in the Chinese people's value system may have profound influences on the elite's ambivalence toward luxury.

Epstein's Cognitive-Experiential Self Theory

In his cognitive-experiential self theory (CEST, 1990),[5] Epstein spoke of the personality as being defined by two parallel interactive systems of information process: a rational system and an experiential system. The rational system operates primarily at the conscious level and is intentional, analytical, primarily verbal, and relatively affect-free. The experiential system is assumed to be automatic, preconscious, holistic, associative, primarily non-verbal, and intimately associated with affect.

These two systems are independent and capable of communicating with and, therefore, influencing each other. Behavior and conscious thought are a joint function of the two systems. The systems normally engage in seamless, integrated interaction, but sometimes they are in conflict. These conflicts are expressed in everyday life as a struggle between feelings and thoughts, between the heart and the mind: "My reason told me to buy the Volkswagen, but my heart told me to buy the Stingray." Conflicts between the rational (analytical) system and the experiential (impulsive) system produce a common dilemma: ordinary brand or luxury brand?

Epstein also proposes that ambivalent attitudes toward luxury goods and consumption exist in every society, whatever an individual's cultural background and social class. But the degree of ambivalence experienced varies according to each individual consumer's social status and cultural context.

China's luxury consumers are experiencing the same mental conflicts, with profound cultural and historical influences. In this chapter, we investigate this issue of attitudinal ambivalence in Mainland China, though relevance of the data, the analysis and the proposed model could be extended to other Asian countries where Confucianism has some influence or in Western countries where some values are in conflict with society.

Attitudes and values

The definitions of, and relationships between, these two concepts should be clarified from the outset. Attitudes are positive or negative standings toward various persons, objects, ideas, or situations. Whereas the definitions and measurements of attitude are widely accepted, values have been a much harder concept to define and measure; three distinct perspectives of values can be delineated.

The first perspective conceptualizes values as special attitudes toward the world because attitudes and values share an evaluative nature. For some,[6] values are simply attitudes toward relatively abstract goals and concepts. Glenn (1980)[7] believes that values are a special kind of attitude—highly abstract ideas about what is good or bad, right or wrong, desirable or undesirable. According to this perspective the difference between attitudes and values is that values give an evaluation of a highly abstract concept, whereas attitudes are evaluations in general. These definitions identify value as a special case of attitude.

A second perspective on the definition of values conceptualizes values as the criteria used in evaluations and behaviors. Kluckhohn (1951)[8] defined values as "a conception of the desirable which influences the selection from available modes, means, and end of action."

Robin Williams (1970)[9] refined this description as "those conceptions of desirable stages of affairs that are utilized in selective conduct as criteria for preference or choice or as justifications for proposed or actual behavior."

The third perspective combines elements of the other two, seeing values as both evaluative and criteria. Hechter (1993)[10] agreed that values and attitudes are similar but argued that values are general and durable, whereas attitudes are particular and transitory. He defined values as "relatively general and durable internal criteria for evaluation." Rokeach (1973)[11] argued that values transcend attitudes toward specific objects and situations:

> A value is an enduring belief that a specific mode of conduct or end-state of existence is personally or socially preferable to other modes of conduct or end-states of existence. A value system is an enduring organization of beliefs concerning preferable modes of conduct or end-states of existence along a continuum of relative importance.

In this definition Rokeach addresses both the evaluative (preferable) and criteria (specific) nature of values. From these definitions it can be argued that attitudes and values are similar in that they are both expressed as evaluations of social objects. However, they are different in that values are more enduring and attitudes more mutable evaluations. Moreover, values are more stable and occupy a more central position than attitudes within a person's cognitive system. Therefore, values are determinants of attitudes and behavior and hence provide us with a more stable and inner-oriented understanding of consumers.[12]

For Rokeach, values and attitudes differ in a number of important respects:

First, whereas a value is a single belief, an attitude refers to an organization of several beliefs that are all focused on a given object or situation.

Second, a value transcends objects and situations, whereas an attitude is focused on some specified objects or situations.

Third, a value is a standard while an attitude is not. Favorable or unfavorable attitudes toward numerous objects and situations may be based upon a relatively small number of values serving as standards.

Fourth, a person accumulates values so far as he gathers beliefs concerning desirable modes of conduct and end-states of existence, but accumulates attitudes with every direct or indirect encounter with specific objects and situations. It is thus estimated that values number only in the dozens, whereas attitudes number in the thousands.

Fifth, values occupy a more central position than attitudes within an individual's personality makeup and cognitive system, and they are therefore determinants of attitudes as well as of behavior.

Sixth, a value is more dynamic than an attitude, having a more immediate link to motivation.

Seventh, the content of a value may be directly relevant to ego defense, knowledge, or self-actualizing functions while the content of an attitude is related to such functions only inferentially.

In our research, the evolution of values in China needs to be analyzed, since conflicting values may lead to ambivalent attitudes. Previous research into values and luxury consumption in China has focused largely on traditional values. Yang (1989),[13] for example, explains Chinese consumer behavior by analyzing the philosophical and religious values—Confucianism, Taoism, and Buddhism—which are fundamental in Chinese history. Zhang and Jolibert (2003)[14] built a scale for these three types of traditional values, while Usunier (1997)[15] discussed Chinese values and luxury goods from a managerial perspective. These aspects of Chinese traditional values need to be further discussed after introducing the "New Ideology" of consumption in China.

Melting-pot value system in transitional China

The Chinese value system is a melting pot combining the values of traditional Chinese culture, religions, and philosophies, and the values of Western cultures, religions, and thoughts.

China is the sole survivor of the four ancient civilizations. Its traditional culture, religions, and philosophies have been the roots of the value systems of the people living in this land for several thousand years. Social morals and virtues, passed down from generation to generation, are the core of a very stable value system against which behavior is evaluated.

In the recent past, from 1840 onward, China experienced violent social change, both from inside and outside. During this period, the country experienced four distinct social systems: the feudal system (from ancient times–1911), the republic (1911–49), the communist system (1949–78), and the post-communist socialist system with Chinese characteristics (1978–today). China is the only country that has experienced so many different social systems during such a short period. Not surprisingly, perhaps, this period has been marked by political instability, violence, internal conflict, external intervention, and invasion.

A better understanding of the social evolution of Chinese society can be gained from a brief consideration of some of the important historical figures, moments, and philosophies that have helped to shape today's China.

Confucius: Cultivate self, then serve the country

Born in 551 BC, Confucius was a teacher, scholar, and political official whose commentary on Chinese literature classics developed into a pragmatic philosophy for daily life. Not strictly religious, the teachings of Confucius were a utilitarian approach advocating social harmony and moral obligations to society. After his death, his followers collected notes on his sayings and doings and recorded them as the *Analects*. His approach was formalized into a political and religious system during the Han dynasty in the early part of the third century. It was embraced by subsequent generations and was the "state religion" of China until the latter part of the 20th century. Max Weber criticized Confucianism on the grounds that its over-reliance on tradition impeded the process of capitalism and industrialization in China.

Qin dynasty (221–207 BC): Chinese unification and the thoughts of Confucianism

The Qin dynasty established the first great Chinese empire and unified the money, writing, and measurement systems. The Qin (from which the name China is derived) established the approximate boundaries and basic administrative system that all subsequent dynasties were to follow. Another Qin accomplishment is the construction of the Great Wall to defend against barbarians from the North. The dynasty is also notorious for burning all non-utilitarian books. From then, Confucianism became the dominant ideology and the fundamental value system of Chinese society for more than 2,000 years.

Han dynasty (206 BC–AD 220): First integration of people and flowering of Chinese culture

The Han dynasty, the second great imperial dynasty, was a period of cultural and artistic flowering. One of the greatest historical documents, the *Shiji* by Sima Qian, was composed, and the *fu*, a poetic form that became the norm for creative writing, began to flourish. Zhang Qian, a military diplomat, convinced the countries in the region of today's Afghanistan to join the Chinese system, thus securing the Silk Road in order to develop and facilitate commerce and exchange with Middle Eastern countries and Europe. Foreign exchanges were initiated and Buddhism was brought into China. Lacquerware, first developed during the Shang dynasty, reached a level of great mastery, and silk was woven for the export trade, which extended as far as Europe. Paper was invented, time was measured with water clocks and sundials, and calendars were published frequently. So thoroughly did the Han dynasty establish what was thereafter considered Chinese culture that the dynasty's very name became the Mandarin Chinese character for the Chinese people.

Tang dynasty (618–907): Elite selection system and expansion of Buddhism

The Tang dynasty succeeded the short-lived Sui dynasty and became a golden age for poetry, sculpture, and Buddhism. The Tang capital of Chang'an became a great international metropolis, with traders and embassies from Central Asia, Arabia, Persia, Korea, and Japan passing through. A Christian community also existed there, while mosques were established in Guangzhou (Canton). The economy flourished in the eighth and ninth centuries, with a network of rural market towns growing up to join the metropolitan markets of Chang'an and Luoyang. Buddhism enjoyed great favor, and there were new translations of Buddhist scriptures and the development of various sects, including Chan. Poetry was the greatest glory of the period; nearly 50,000 works by 2,000 poets have survived. Foreign music and dance became popular, and ancient orchestras were revived. The Tang government developed the national exam system established by its predecessor to attract and select talented young people to enter the government system and help the emperor manage his country. This excellent system of human resource continues today.

Zheng He and his voyage: Prosperity and luxury of the Middle Empire

In the early days of the Ming dynasty (1368–1644), China was the most economically and technologically advanced country in the world. Zheng He, a eunuch also known as San Bao, acting on the orders of the emperor, Zhu Di, led a vast fleet to establish relations with foreign countries, to expand trade, and to look for treasures to satisfy the desire of the sovereign for luxuries. Under his command were 62 ships, manned by more than 27,800 men, including sailors, clerks, interpreters, officials and soldiers, artisans, medical men, and meteorologists. On board were large quantities of cargo that could be broken down into over 40 different categories, including silk goods, porcelain, gold and silver ware, copper utensils, iron implements, cotton goods, mercury, umbrellas, and straw mats. The fleet sailed along the coast of Fujian and, after crossing the South China Sea and the Indian Ocean, reached Java, Sri Lanka, India, Malaysia, Yemen, Iran, Mecca, and, further west, to East Africa. In all, he made calls at more than 30 countries and territories during his eight voyages and all of this half a century before Columbus's voyage to America.

On each voyage Zheng He was acting as the envoy and commercial representative of the Ming court. He called on the ruler of each land he visited, presenting valuable gifts in token of China's sincere desire to develop friendly relations and inviting the host sovereign to send emissaries to China. Wherever he went, he made a careful study of the customs and habits of local residents. Showing them due respect, he bartered or dealt with them through consultation and negotiation on the basis of equality and mutual benefit. In this way, he obtained large quantities of pearls and precious stones, coral, ivory, and dyestuffs for the emperor. He also brought back several exotic animals including giraffe, lion, ostrich, and leopard.

The countries Zheng He visited later sent their emissaries and trade representatives to China, where they were shown great hospitality. The voyages by Zheng He strengthened the friendly relations between China and other countries in Asia and Africa and provided the impetus for cultural and economic exchange.

Qing dynasty (1644–1911): Conservatism, extravagance, and corruption

During the last imperial dynasties, China's territory and population expanded tremendously. The Manchu, believing the Han culture to be the best, most advanced system, refused any evolutions in philosophy, thought, economy, and technology. The cultural attitudes were strongly conservative, dominated by Neo-Confucianism. However, hedonism was very well developed. The arts flourished: the literati painting[16] was popular, novels in the vernacular developed substantially, and *jingxi* (Peking opera) developed. Qing porcelain, textiles, tea, paper, sugar, and steel were exported to all parts of the world. But the feudal political system was no longer suited to the social evolution and economic development of the country. Nothing was done to develop technology to improve productivity, and commerce was constrained. Thus, China missed the opportunities of industrialization and fell behind developing European countries, such as Portugal, Spain, Holland, and England.

Military campaigns in the latter part of the 18th century depleted government finances and corruption grew. The imperial consort, Cixi, confiscated a year's naval budget to build the Summer Palace for her birthday. These conditions, combined with population pressures and natural disasters, led to the Opium Wars and the Taiping and Nian rebellions, which in turn so weakened the dynasty that it was unable to rebuff the demands of foreign powers.

First Opium War and the Treaty of Nanjing: Collapse of feudal China

China had engaged in trade with Western countries since the late 16th century. The Chinese, accustomed to tributary relationships with others, required that Westerners pay for goods with silver. To offset a growing negative flow of silver at home, the British began importing it into China illegally. As demand for opium grew, China tried to stop the practice, and hostilities broke out in 1840. Britain quickly triumphed, and the resultant Treaty of Nanjing was a blow to China. The outbreak of a second war with an Anglo-French alliance resulted in the Treaty of Tianjin (1858), which required further Chinese concessions. When China refused to sign subsequent treaties, Beijing (Peking) was captured and the emperor's summer palace burned. The overall result of these conflicts was to weaken the Chinese imperial system, greatly expand Western influence in China, and pave the way for such uprisings as the Taiping and Boxer rebellions.

The Treaty of Nanking is the first of the Unequal Treaties signed by China with a foreign country. Under the treaty, China agreed to cede Hong Kong to the British, and open a number of its ports—Canton (Guangzhou),

Dalian, Shanghai, Qingdao, and Tianjin—to foreign trade with low tariffs. (These port cities were the first open to the world and we can see the influence of this early opening: people in these cities are very familiar with Western lifestyles and have a positive attitude toward foreign products.) Thereafter, the opium trade flourished, and Hong Kong developed rapidly as an Anglo-Chinese enclave, until the British transferred sovereignty of Hong Kong and the leased territories back to China in 1997.

Xin Hai Revolution and May 4th Movement: Renaissance of freedom, democracy and science

The Qing dynasty ended with the republican revolution of 1911 (Xin Hai Revolution) and the abdication of the last emperor in 1912, following which China switched from being an autocratic monarchy to a modern country. After the First World War, on May 4, 1919, Beijing students demonstrated in Tiananmen Square against the Treaty of Versailles, which transferred German concessions in Shandong to Japan rather than returning sovereign authority to China. As a result of the students' actions, China withdrew from the Treaty and the demand for freedom, democracy, and science led to a renaissance of the Chinese people.

Japanese invasion and Second World War: Renaissance of nationalism and people

The Japanese invasion of China began in September 1931 when the Japanese army occupied Manchuria and established the puppet state of Manchukuo the following year. In July 1937, a clash between soldiers of the Japanese garrison in Beijing and Chinese forces at the Marco Polo Bridge was the pretext for Japanese occupation of Beijing and Tianjin. Chiang Kai-shek refused to negotiate on Japanese terms and, after a protracted struggle, Shanghai and the national capital, Nanjing, fell to the Japanese. The subsequent killing of 300,000 civilians in Nanjing is well recorded.

The Japanese bombing of Pearl Harbor brought the United States into the war and China declared war on Japan, Germany, and Italy. Japan was forced to divert its forces elsewhere and, with U.S. and British aid, China eventually forced the surrender of Japanese troops in September 1945. By the provisions of the Cairo Declaration, Manchuria, Taiwan, and the Pescadores were restored to China.

During this period, Chinese nationalism developed strongly and victory over the Japanese boosted national confidence to resist foreign invasion and stop the repetition of past failures. However, the war sapped the nationalist government's strength, while allowing Communist guerrilla units to gain control over large areas of the country, which led to the final overthrow of the nationalist government in 1949. Another enduring legacy of the war against Japan is the continuing antipathy toward Japan and its products.

Foundation of Communist China: Marxism and Maoism

After four years of civil war with the KMT (Kuo Min Tang), the Communists founded the People's Republic of China in 1949. The nationalists withdrew to the island of Taiwan. Mao established the communist social system and Marxist ideology on the Mainland. By the end of the 1950s, and under Mao's guidance, the nationalization of private capital was largely complete. However, vestiges of old wealth and heritage wealth still remained in cities such as Tianjin, Shanghai, Guangzhou, Dalian, Qingdao, Beijing, Wuhan, and other major centers, but these were removed and further social and political changes were introduced.

Cultural Revolution (1966–76): Anti-intellectual, anti-bourgeois

The Cultural Revolution resulted in a decade of social turmoil and China's economic development experienced its most severe setback since the founding of the People's Republic. This was brought about by the mass

mobilization of urban youth by Mao Zedong in an attempt to prevent
the development of a bureaucratized, Soviet-style of Communism. Mao
closed schools and encouraged students to join Red Guard units, which
denounced and persecuted Chinese teachers and intellectuals, engaged
in widespread book burning, facilitated mass relocations, and enforced
Mao's cult of personality. The criticism of party officials, intellectuals,
and "bourgeois values" turned violent, and the Red Guard split into fac-
tions. Torture was commonplace, and it is estimated that a million died
in the ensuing purges and related incidents. The Cultural Revolution
also caused economic disruption; industrial production dropped by 12%
from 1966 to 1968. In 1971, Mao expressed regrets for the excesses of
the Cultural Revolution. However, the Gang of Four, led by Jiang Qing,
continued to restrict the arts and enforce ideology, even purging Deng
Xiaoping a second time only months before Mao's death in September
1976. The members of the Gang of Four were imprisoned in October
1976, bringing a period of turmoil to a close.

The Culture Revolution had a profound impact on Chinese society,
the effects of which are still being felt today (see the generation profiles in Chapter 1). In addition to the enormous economic and industrial
disruption, the Cultural Revolution demolished traditional culture and
social harmony and replaced them with communist catchwords and slo-
gans. Communist ideology and values had become embedded into the
minds of the Chinese people. By the end of the Cultural Revolution, economic recession and the paralysis of industrial production had reduced
the Chinese people to extreme poverty. Old wealth and heritage wealth
had been obliterated, which is why the affluent, wealthy, and super-rich
in today's Mainland China are all "new rich" and share most of the common characteristics and behaviors of their counterparts in the West.

Reform and opening to the West

In December 1978, the central government made the strategic decision
to undertake a socialist modernization program, reforming the outdated

economic system, revitalizing the domestic economy, and opening up to the outside world. The national exam system was re-established to select talented young people to receive university education. The Fourteenth National Congress of the Communist Party of China set the goal of establishing a socialist market economy.

In January 1979, the United States and China agreed to recognize each other and to establish diplomatic relations. Since then, bilateral trade has expanded a hundredfold and joint ventures have proliferated. In less than three decades, China's economy has undergone a fundamental change from a planned economy to a market economy. As the country's economic strength intensified, the living standards of its people improved. The annual GDP growth rate has remained steady at around 9% since 1979, with per-capita income rising above US$2,000 in 2006. China was in a phase of re-establishment in every field. Along with political and economic change have come changes in all aspects of Chinese society, culture, and education, which have seen a uniquely Chinese value system which mixes traditional, Communist, and Western values.

WTO: Integration into the world economy

In December 2001, China officially became the 143rd member of the World Trade Organization (WTO). Up until that time, and despite the undoubted success of the reform and opening policy, the Chinese did not feel really integrated with the world economy and respected by their counterparts. Since then, however, China has become the focus of world attention, with thousands of foreign companies scrambling to take advantage of its cheap labor, cheap industrial land, and educated workforce by relocating their manufacturing and distribution centers to China. It is an ideal production center for businesses based in outside countries. Western countries benefit from access to China's highly developed electronics and industry sectors. With duties and quotas slashed, and restrictions lifted, multinationals benefit by setting up distribution centers without the need for Chinese middlemen.

Gaining entrance to the WTO has given Chinese businessmen greater confidence in moving into businesses abroad, as can be seen in Lenovo's acquisition of IBM personal PC activities, in the TCL-Thomson Alliance, in Hair's manufacture platform in South Carolina, and in Chery's success in selling cars in Europe.

Chinese in space: Patriotism and new technology

In October 2003, China became the third country to send an astronaut into space. Since then, it has been actively planning its deep space exploration over the next few years, focusing on lunar and Mars exploration. China's willingness to explore space and study the distribution and utilization of lunar resources and terrestrial planetary science, as well as exploring scientific measures for supporting mankind's sustainable survival on Earth, shows that it is becoming a world superpower. Its successful launch into space exploration has served to reinforce the patriotism of the Mainland Chinese and overseas Chinese in every corner of the world.

Another positive impact of this venture has been the improvement in the image of Chinese-made products around the world. New technology and industrial products have started to pour into the world market, in both developing and industrialized countries alike. Many Chinese enterprises—ZTE, Huawei electronics, and TCL, to name but a few—are benefiting from this.

Olympic Games: Internationalization and returning to the world

Beijing winning the right to host the 2008 Olympic Games will help China deepen its re-integration into the world and will focus the world's attention on what China has to offer.

As China is becoming more self-confident on the world stage, so are its people, and this is bringing about changes in Chinese consumers. New wealthy people are willing to try the high-end products and services enjoyed by their Western counterparts and luxury goods are becoming an indispensable part of their lives.

From this brief review of some of the more recent historical events and social movements, it is clear that China's value system is no longer like the traditional image of the popular imagination. Although some of the traditional values remain to underpin the new value system, after more than half a century of Chinese Communist Party rule communist and post-communist values occupy a dominant position in that system. And, with economic development, Western values are exerting greater influence, particularly in the area of cultural products and services (Hollywood films and MTV, for example) for young people.

"Melting-pot" is an appropriate description of China's value systems today. The values in the pot are having an influence on the behavior of luxury consumers and can explain more explicitly the luxury consumption of the Chinese elite.

The persistence of traditional values

In the studies conducted into the Chinese value system, traditional values and consumption in China have been looked at from a sociological and philosophical perspective[17] or from a methodological viewpoint in order to build scales of traditional values.[18] Some researchers have employed values surveys,[19] or international comparisons of marketing practices such as communication and advertising (Chu and Ju, 1993;[20] Cheng and Schweitzer, 1996;[21] Lin, 2001[22]).

As mentioned earlier, some researchers have classified Chinese consumers into three religious philosophical groups: Confucianism, Taoism, and Buddhism.[23] Zhang and Jolibert developed scales of Confucianism (with social status, family, respect, listening to others), Taoism (with respect of nature and harmony with nature) and Buddhism (with justice, predestination, uselessness of luxury, and so on). However, as the authors acknowledge, these scales do not take into account Western values, which also have an influence on China. Neither do they incorporate the "new ideology" values related to modernity and wealth.

My objective here is to integrate traditional and "new" sources of values corresponding to the current reality of Chinese society in the 21st century. Of all the traditional values, which are still prominent today?

Studies of the traditional values of affluent Chinese are based on a Chinese Values Survey (CVS), which identified 40 traditional cultural values.[24] However, more recent studies of contemporary Chinese culture have found that, while the Chinese heritage was of great importance in shaping the way it encounters modernity,[25] only part of those traditional values are prevalent in the present situation.[26]

The changes in China are rooted in social evolutions such as the introduction of modern values into Chinese cultural and ideological systems through, for example, the implementation of Marxism and Maoism or the theory of Deng. Among the remaining traditional values are those we might consider as virtues (family, economy/frugality, modesty/humility, perseverance) as opposed to those related to social behavior (face-saving, interdependence/collectivism, and patriotism).[27] These values, rated as strong and prevalent, persist in today's Chinese society and they influence consumption, and hence the attitudes toward luxury goods.

Tradition is one of the most important values in 18 traditional Chinese cultural values identified in the CVS.[28] The value "Tradition" is not only consonant with the contemporary mentality of the Chinese, but is also part of the national heritage itself. In general, tradition embraces a series of values that belong to traditional virtues and traditional social behavior.

Family

This is the strongest of the values identified because families are regarded as societal cells and the harmony of families is deemed essential for maintaining social stability. This is as true today as it was in the past. TV commercials with "family" as the dominant theme are very appealing to Chinese consumers,[29] and this is utilized by the mass-market brands, such as P&G and Hitachi, to get larger media coverage and closer communication with their clients. The most successful TV commercial for a luxury product is a Rémy Martin ad in which a family is shown having dinner and playing mahjong together in a very convivial environment. When they open a bottle of Rémy Martin cognac, one of them wins the game and everyone is very happy. The tag line—"Once the Re Tou Ma (Rémy Martin's Chinese name) is open, good luck comes naturally"— reinforces the positive images. Rémy Martin put its cognac consumption in a Chinese family context and associates this with good luck for family members. In so doing, it succeeds in reducing the psychological distance between the ordinary Chinese luxury consumer and an imported Western luxury product.

Confucianism places great importance on family relationships and their implicit responsibilities and rewards. The individual is ready and willing to make sacrifices for his family and, in exchange, expects his family to be there as his support, comfort, and safety net. The individual is taught to put family members before self, to share their pride and accomplishments, their shame and their failure, their sadness and their joy as if they were his own. This intense relationship with the family is a lifelong affair. The family relationship of mutual aid and dependence is a permanent one and also extends to grandparents, aunts, uncles, cousins, and so on.[30]

Chinese luxury consumers, like their Western counterparts, often buy their family members luxury products on special occasions, such as Spring Festival, birthdays, and promotions. Their logic is that if their financial situation has improved through professional or business success, they should share the results with parents, help relatives to improve their situation, or help finance their siblings' educations and business. In return, the successful giver is accorded greater respect by the family members, while bringing pride and glory to their parents and relatives. This is much more important than the wealth itself. Professional achievement and political success can also bring pride and glory to family and the respect that comes with it can also be extended to the rest of the family. Thus, the family plays a substantial role in luxury consumption in China.

Economy/Frugality

In traditional Chinese culture and history, philosophers and scholars have expressed their opinions on frugality/economy and luxury ("luxury" here is the Chinese "*shē chǐ*", meaning "extravagance", as discussed in Chapter 2). Their recorded thoughts, classical works passed down through thousands of years, include aphorisms such as "frugality, the common point of virtue; luxury, the worst of sins"[31] and "frugality and simplicity is beautiful,"[32] became the foundation of social norms and ethical behavior. With these views transmitted and reinforced by the scholar-bureaucrats over many centuries, extravagance and waste were to be avoided at all levels of society: people were to be frugal in their daily lives, modest and discreet in their behavior and attitudes, even if they were super-rich and high-level statesmen.

It comes as a surprise to some when the super-rich do exercise frugality. Take the case of Madame Gong Ruxin who died recently, leaving a fortune of US$4.2 billion. Her story made headlines when it was discovered that her monthly expenses amounted to no more US$400 and, despite her vast wealth, she never bought luxury goods. Her favorite food was McDonald's Filet-O-Fish and her preference was for Chinese traditional and leisure clothing. Though they are often referred to as misers, the super-rich who exercise restraint and frugality are merely showing adherence to long-standing traditional values, which condemn conspicuous displays of wealth and power.

Modesty/Humility

The modesty and humility encouraged by Confucianism are captured in a famous Chinese proverb dating back several thousand years: "Modesty helps one to go forward, whereas conceit makes one lag behind."[33] These are an essential part of the social criteria necessary to maintain social stability and durable governance. Three cardinal guides for traditional Chinese society were: ruler guides subject, father guides son, and husband guides wife (君为臣纲，父为子纲，夫为妻纲). While Confucian doctrines such as this may have been useful for ensuring social stability, Weber (1963, 1974)[34] found that they also hindered the development of capitalism in modern China.

The influence of modesty and humility on luxury consumption is complex. On the surface, the direct impact may be negative in that people tend to weigh frugality over luxury. However, frugality might also find expression in the way luxury is consumed. For example, some luxury consumers buy the luxury brands very discreetly and their usage is very personal and private, not given to extravagant public display. This is perhaps seen in their preference for the Bentley over its sister brand, the Rolls-Royce. The flying-lady logo seems to be too much for China's super-rich, symbolizing extreme power as exercised by the likes of emperors and kings: in socialist China, nobody wants to seem to be challenging the rule of the Communist Party. The comparative discretion and modesty of the Bentley is more suited to the mentality of China's super-rich.

Perseverance[35]

Fortitude is a key driver in accomplishing great feats, and characteristic of prominent heroes throughout Chinese history. Perseverance is a value that has rated highly in previous studies of Chinese values[36] and one which can influence attitudes to consumption. How this has influenced attitudes toward luxury consumption is still unknown, though perseverance is coherent with excellence and quality, two of the hallmarks of the luxury industry.

Saving face

This is an important cultural phenomenon within Chinese society and a great deal has been published on the subject. It revolves around the notion of gaining and maintaining the respect of others and thus influences every aspect of consumer behavior.[37] It is social rather than personal in nature. Where pride is personal, face is public. It is the desire to not appear weak or look bad in the eyes of others. It is not necessarily about how an individual *is*, but how he *is viewed* by others.

If we put this into a wider historical context of modern Asian history, this may help explain the Asian fever for luxury brands. For a very long time, Asian countries, especially those influenced by Chinese culture, were invaded or occupied by Western powers. But they were not conquered mentally. When their situations changed, buying luxury brands was one way to show that they were no longer weak, to display to all their status.

As we saw in Chapter 1, for the Chinese, respect is the key element by which they can show their standing in society. Respect and saving face are closely connected. In Chinese traditional culture, to challenge a person or his opinion is to show no respect toward that person. That is why it is rare to hear an inferior say no to a superior.

Face-saving behavior is essentially a compromise (the English have something similar in their notion of "gentlemanly conduct"). It allows foes to meet in the middle ground. You can compete with a person but you must be careful to maintain his face. If you make him lose face in front of others, however, you had better be prepared to go all the way because he will have no recourse but to attack you. This is perhaps best seen in the Japanese Samurai concept of hara-kiri, where death is preferable to the humiliation of defeat.

The influence of saving face in luxury consumption is both wide and important. In a survey conducted by the *China Youth Daily* in 2005, 87% of respondents agreed that saving face was an integral part of their lives. This is a collective value and saving face is all about collective living in society. If purchasing a certain luxury brand can give or save face through, for example, showing that they are elegant or have good taste, then that brand will be well accepted by Chinese luxury consumers.

The face-saving, collective mentality of the Chinese leads to imitation behavior in consumption, and this can be exploited in various ways through different marketing strategies. This may explain why certain luxury brands are sought-after while their competitors are not well accepted.

Collectivism

Collectivism is defined as one of the five aspects of Chinese tradition that possibly relates to luxury consumption.[38] It is based on the fundamental connection of human beings and the idea that the individual's identity lies in family, cultural, professional, and social relationships. Interdependence is a collective value. For the Chinese, status/class is not simply a question of individual achievement; it also reflects the position of one's group, family, relatives, and kinship clan.[39]

The Chinese feel that individual behavior should be guided by the expectations of the group. Confucianism was essentially an elaboration on the obligations between emperor and subject, parent and child, husband and wife, older brother and younger brother, and between friends. Chinese society made the individual feel very much a part of a large, complex, and generally benign social organism in which prescriptive obligations of various relationships were a guide to ethical conduct.[40] This emphasis on the collective resulted in the Chinese valuing in-group harmony. Within the social group, any form of confrontation was discouraged. Debate was not encouraged and one person could not contradict another without fear of making an enemy,[41] which is why saving face—both for self and others—is so crucial for maintaining harmony within the group. Thus the opinion of the collective becomes crucial in Chinese society.

Whether luxury consumption is accepted by Chinese society and its social moral standards is one of the keys to Chinese luxury consumption in the long run. The most practical influence of the collective mentality on luxury consumption is that if a luxury brand has high, positive, brand awareness, it will create a push effect within the wider collective, where face-saving behavior will ensure that others follow the lead. A perfect example of how this works can be seen in the experience of the Lacoste brand in China.

Lacoste began its accessible luxury business in the 1980s and decades of effort have resulted in very high brand awareness. According to *Time* magazine's global luxury survey in 2007, Lacoste is second only to Rolex in luxury brand awareness in China. Although it has suffered very much from counterfeiting in the market, it is considered to be the leisure wear of "big bosses." Thus, all bosses or those who aspire to become a boss would want to buy a distinctively colored shirt to give them face. Louis Vuitton fulfills a similar role for young girls and female office workers.

Patriotism

From ancient times, patriotism has been a strong value in Chinese tradition. In his poem "Testament for my son", Lu You (1127–1279) wrote:

> After my death I know for me all hopes are vain, but still I'm grieved to see our country not united. When Royal Armies recover the heartland, do not forget to tell your Sire in sacred rite!

This strength of patriotic feeling has been encouraged throughout the ages by emperors, landlords, republicans, and communists alike in an effort to unify the Chinese against common enemies and maintain stability.

This value persists widely in Chinese consumers of all ages, whether in urban or rural areas[42] and is reflected widely in advertising.[43] It is linked with protectionism, which influences the consumer's attitude toward foreign-made products.[44] However, the luxury consumer's attitudes toward Western luxury goods—for which there are currently no viable Chinese alternatives—are generally positive and do not appear to have been affected by patriotism. However, the clothing of the Tang dynasty and other traditional dress is coming back into fashion and some of the social elite adopt traditional clothing for public events. The traditional Chinese style and colors made by the Shanghai Tang company are currently very successful and this trend is developing very quickly both in China and in overseas-Chinese markets.

New ideological values

Since the late 1970s, the reform and opening policy has seen the Communist planned economy transformed into a market-oriented economy. Economic development, with its "Four Modernizations" (in agriculture, industry, science and technology, and national defense), has become the central task for China's leaders. Opening to the outside world has entailed the acceptance of advanced technologies and achievements from around the world and, therefore, the adoption of some modern, foreign values.

In 1985, Deng acknowledged that "China has no alternative but to follow this road; it is the only road to prosperity" and in 1990 he said: "We should seize every opportunity to develop the economy." Through following this policy, the Chinese economy has developed remarkably and people's living conditions have improved considerably, particularly in the big cities.

As a result, a "new ideology" of consumption has emerged and materialistic attitudes and behavior are evident in modern Chinese society. The values of this new ideology extracted from Deng's theories—modernity, success, wealth, social position, confidence, and leadership—are embodied in the attitudes and behavior of the Chinese elite, the luxury goods consumers.

Modernity

Modernity is regarded as future-oriented, emphasizing the notion of being new, up-to-date, and ahead of time. In today's China this is manifest in the adoption of management and marketing skills as well as advanced science and technology from advanced industrialized countries.[45] A modern society is defined as having a very high level of differentiation, urbanization, high literacy, and wide exposure to the mass media. It is culturally dynamic and oriented toward change and innovation.[46] After 150 years of wars, instability, and political and social upheaval, people are eager to enjoy the stability and affluence that modernization should bring.

For the Chinese, modernization means a better life and the hope of prosperity. Old cities are being reconstructed, with traditional houses giving way to high-rise apartments, shopping malls, and highways. The traditional now seems to represent the old China and is seen as being behind the times. New technologies and industrialization are the means by which China will keep pace with the world. The launch of the space-craft Shenzhou V sent a signal to the world and to the Chinese themselves that China has become a modern and technologically advanced country and has washed off past humiliations at the hands of foreign invaders. Thus, modernization is a very positive value in China. All things modern are quickly accepted by Chinese consumers.

To the Chinese mind, Western-made products represent modernity and the big multinational companies have enjoyed tremendous success in China with good-quality products that meet the needs of consumers.

Luxury brands, many of which blend tradition with modernity, represent the essence of modern society to the Chinese consumer. The values they embody are seen to transfer to the person who buys them. Thus, the more you know about the luxury brands and the more luxury products you possess, the more you project a modern image to friends, colleagues, and members of your social network. This is the dominant value of current Chinese society and is likely to remain so for a long time to come.

The argument that a modern society will be more homogenous arises from the assumption that modern society must approximate to a single type—the Western type. However, modernization is not the same thing as Westernization. Modern Asian cultures are, and will remain, profoundly Asian.[47] A modern China will still be China. The traditional values at the core of Chinese society, as described earlier, will endure.

A luxury brand starting up in China needs to build brand awareness based on its Western identity, culture, and values, using the same communication strategies as it employed in its home country. Once strong brand awareness has been established, it should integrate some Chinese elements into its local and global communication. For example, in 2006, Louis Vuitton invited Du Juan, a top Chinese model, to join its worldwide advertising campaign, the first time it had ever used an Asian face in its worldwide brand communication. In 2007, Hermès organized an exposition at the Shanghai Art Museum of Carré design, featuring the work of Chinese designers. In October of the same year, Fendi held a fashion show on the Great Wall in Beijing. This was the biggest fashion industry show in the world. The strong traditional background presented an opportunity for Chinese brands to grow. The potential market is colossal.

Success/Achievement

For the Chinese elite, success is a very important goal, and one linked to the consumption of luxury goods. Achievement is also one of two key elements that create vanity, strongly linked with conspicuous consumption.[48]

Schütte pointed out that in the Western context the need for achievement is related to the need for both socially directed prestige and for personally directed self-realization. People with a need for achievement tend to be more self-confident, enjoy taking calculated risks, are very sensitive to new products or ventures, and are very interested in feedback. Products and services that signify success are particularly appealing as they provide feedback to the individuals about the realization of their goals. Luxury products which have become associated with achievement include cigars, champagne and spirits, limousines, watches, and yachts, which are seen as rewards for success.

For Chinese consumers, achievement is a primary means of satisfying the social need for admiration from their communities, as well as showing status in society at large. The self-satisfaction that achievement brings to individual Chinese comes not because it sets them above the group, but because of the social status and respect that it brings. In other words, achievement in the Asian context is very much a socially directed need, in contrast to the personally directed self-realization needs of Western consumers. Luxury brands can meet perfectly the needs of Chinese consumers to be respected by others through the actions of buying, possessing, and consuming those brands.

Wealth

Wealth is often correlated with success. The importance of gaining social recognition in a collective society has turned Asians into probably the most image-conscious consumers in the world. Some 70% of respondents in a study in East Asian countries indicated that earning a great deal of money and acquiring luxury goods (particularly expensive cars) are among the most important goals in life.[49]

Consumers with a positive attitude toward money and wealth are seeking to become rich.[50] Deng Xiaoping's statement that "To be wealthy is a glorious thing"[51] is clearly embedded in China's new ideology. Luxury products are the symbols of wealth and power and the objects of conspicuous consumption. This fits perfectly well with the current situation in China, where to get rich is highly encouraged and to be one of the new rich is glorious.

Rupert Hoogewerf, is the founder and compiler of the annual Hurun China Rich List. This acts as a billboard of wealth, showing who earns the most money and the business sectors in which they operate. It is a direct encouragement of the bold pursuit of money and pushes money-oriented values onto the Chinese public. At the same time, however, it also sets in train an anti-rich sentiment. The economic spoils that development brings are not shared equally by all: the majority of Chinese are still embroiled in the struggle to achieve a modestly affluent life. The high unemployment in middle and small cities and in the countryside and the lack of social security create social problems that are yet to come to a head. People like this are left wondering where those on the rich list get their money from.

Since Hoogewerf's list was first published in 1999, the names have changed almost every year and this has drawn the attention of the Chinese government and led to investigations into the legitimacy of such wealth acquisition. While some who have disappeared from the list are now in jail for engaging in illegal activities, the changes also give a clear indication of the rapidity with which new wealth is being created.

To calm public disquiet regarding the sources of their wealth, the super-rich have become increasingly involved in charities; to strike a balance between wealth and social harmony. A similar problem confronts luxury brands and the behavior of luxury consumers: how to achieve equilibrium among conflicting values.

Social position

Since the pursuit of wealth was first encouraged after the reform and opening policy, people have become increasingly sensitive to the need to improve their financial situation as a means of improving their social standing. A better life should have a material basis: money becomes the key element for the new classification of social categories. As the rich have a higher social position than the poor, they command more face and respect. The collective recognition of success and achievement brings glory to the individual and to his/her family.

Conspicuous consumption is one of the typical and label behaviors of the leisure class (to use Veblen's phrase) and is imitated by people who aspire to join that class. The leisure class in China is emerging. The Chinese elite (as defined in Chapter 1) are achieving professional success and acquiring new wealth based on very high educational achievement and family environment. Their social position is such that they are not the most sensitive group to social position. In fact, those whom I have referred to as the "vulgar rich" and the lower-middle working class are more sensitive to social distinction and seek to be classified as elite. They imitate and amplify the consumption behaviors of the elite, underlining the fact that social position is an important driver and motivation for the consumption of luxury goods.

Confidence

The confidence of the young Chinese elite comes from two things: pride in China's heritage and an increasingly solid socio-economic base. With economic development, China's confidence has increased and is reflected in international events such as being admitted into the WTO, winning the right to host the 2008 Olympic Games, and hosting the 2010 World Exposition in Shanghai.

This increase in self-confidence has led Chinese people to consume more and travel more. By the end of 2006, 132 countries and regions were welcoming Chinese citizens and hoping to benefit from the fruits of this country's 25 years of economic development. The signing of the CEPA[52] agreement with Hong Kong and the tourism agreement with the European Union[53] has given further impetus to this movement. Today, Chinese tourists swarm into countries such as Thailand, Malaysia, and Singapore, crowding the luxury product shops.

TABLE 3.1: *Chinese government's approved-destination status (ADS) countries*

Asia	Thailand, Singapore, Malaysia, Indonesia, the Philippines, Cambodia, Brunei, Myanmar, Laos, Vietnam, Japan, the Republic of Korea, India, Sri Lanka, Pakistan, Nepal, Turkey, Jordan, Maldives, Mariana, Mongolia, Bengal, United Arab Emirates
Oceania	Australia, New Zealand, Fiji
Europe	Malta, Russia, Hungary, Germany, France, Italy, the Netherlands, Greece, Spain, Portugal, Austria, Sweden, Switzerland, Finland, Belgium, Luxembourg, Croatia, Czech, Denmark, Estonia, Latvia, Lithuania, Poland, Slovenia, Slovak, Cyprus, Iceland, Ireland, Norway, Romania, Liechtenstein, Britain, Andorra
Africa	Egypt, South Africa, Morocco, Ethiopia, Zimbabwe, Tanzania, Mauritius, Tunisia, Kenya, Zambia, Lesotho, Botswana, Madagascar, Namibia, Ghana, Gabon, Mali, Benin, Cameroon, Rwanda, Mozambique, Nigeria, Algeria, Uganda
Americas	Cuba, Chile, Jamaica, Brazil, Mexico, Peru, Antigua, Barbados, Saint-Louisa, Ecuador, Uruguay, Venezuela, Argentina, Trinidad and Tobago

Source: *China National Tourism Administration (CNTA), April 2007.*

Traveling to Europe to experience European cultures is becoming a trendy activity for Chinese consumers, particularly young couples, successful businessmen, and mid-level government officials. Chinese travelers are also discovering the best products and services, filling the luxury product shops in Paris, London, Frankfurt, and Rome, and the

DFS outlets in airports all over the world. Some 20% of the customers at the Louis Vuitton boutique on the Champs-Elysées in Paris are Chinese from Hong Kong, Taiwan, Malaysia, and the Mainland. This percentage is increasing every year as more and more Mainlanders take to the skies.[54]

Leadership

Leadership is a core value reflected in Mao Zedong and Deng Xiaoping's theories to motivate the Chinese people to march toward a common goal with a sense of unity.[55] This value is motivating Chinese people to be independent in their thinking and to overcome difficulties. The spirit underlying the saying "Better to be the head of a dog than the tail of a lion" is a common rule of organizational behavior in China. However, this value may be something of a double-edged sword for Western luxury brands. On one hand, leadership pushes and influences Chinese consumers to enjoy the best products in the world. On the other hand, though, it is associated with confidence and patriotism, creating a desire to build our own Chinese brands. While Chinese luxury brands have yet to become a reality, the spirit of leadership of Mao and Deng provides the moral guidance to ensure that this will happen in the not-too-distant future.

In the melting-pot of value systems in 21st-century China, the new ideology is the dominant force in shaping Chinese society.

Western values influence people to express their personal tastes

Previous cross-cultural studies have shown that strong Western cultural values influence Chinese consumer behavior and are also manifest in Chinese television commercials.[56] Though three modern values (youth, modernity, and individualism) have been classified as newly found values resulting from Western influences in Chinese culture, two of, these—youth and modernity—were, in fact, introduced as part of Deng's new ideology and are not the result of Westernization. It is worth repeating the point raised earlier: modern civilization does not necessarily mean Western civilization.

Asian countries have their own distinct cultural heritage and have followed a different path toward modernization; they will never be replicas of the West. A century of modernization cannot erase thousands of years of cultural heritage.

Nevertheless, Western values such as individualism and personal freedom have gradually taken root among Chinese consumers, most notably among urban youth, and will strengthen as China becomes more integrated into the world economic system.

Economic hubs such as Shanghai, Beijing, Guangzhou, and Chengdu are becoming increasingly cosmopolitan. Young people learn English in schools and universities and are able to access large amounts of information in English via the Internet and satellite TV. As foreign investment pours into China, living conditions show considerable improvement.

As they are exposed to Western influences through work and travel, building professional and social networks along the way, the Chinese elite are increasingly at ease with Western lifestyles. The greater individualism and personal freedom they demonstrate in their daily lives, including their consumption of luxury goods, are becoming more accepted in Chinese society at large.

Individualism

Geert Hofstede has described individualistic societies as those in which the ties between individuals are loose: individuals are expected to look after themselves and their immediate family.[57]

Although many more Chinese are coming into contact with Western values on a day-to-day basis, individualism is not publicly encouraged in Chinese society. For example, in primary schools, the emphasis in education is still on collectiveness and respect for the common interests of society. In traditional Chinese culture, individualism can only be tolerated on condition that the individualistic behavior remains personal and has no influence on collective interests and does not conflict with social moral standards. In communist theory, individualism is totally rejected because it challenges the common interests of the collective.

However, individualism is being used to attract the attention of young consumers and encourage them to express freely their own tastes. A recent commercial for China Mobile's M-Zone service, for example, has the slogan "My zone, I decide." To date, though, the promotion of individualism has been limited and is tolerated only unofficially.

Personal freedom

This is obviously linked with individualism and opposes the interdependence and collectiveness of traditional Chinese values. Personal freedom in consumer behavior means making choices on the basis of personal preference, without considering what others think.

In direct contradiction to the doctrines of traditional Chinese society, communist Chinese society, and post-communist Chinese society, this value encourages people to express themselves freely in words, writing, painting, music, clothes, lifestyles, and so on. It has never been formally accepted by the authorities of China. However, personal freedom is an important value influencing luxury consumer behavior and the creation of luxury products.

Every season, talented designers give free expression to their thoughts and tastes through their work, and luxury consumers express their own tastes and attitudes toward life through the clothes and accessories they buy, without regard to the collective thinking of society. Thus, in China, the degree to which this value gains social acceptance will largely influence luxury consumption and product choices. As we will see in Chapter 5, the extravagant and the discreet will be clearly differentiated by different groups of consumers with different value orientations.

In summary, then, modern China is a melting pot into which conflicting value systems—traditional and new, Chinese and Western—have been thrown together.

Some of these values favor luxury consumption while others could be seen to work against it. These conflicting values serve to create a psychological ambivalence in the minds of luxury consumers and influence their consumption behavior.

ENDNOTES

1   Dubois and Laurent, 1996, "Le Luxe par delà les frontiers: une étude exploratoire dans douze pays", *Décisions Marketing*, No. 9, Sept–Dec., pp.35–43.

2   Nyeck and Roux, 2003, "Valeurs Culturelles et Attitudes par rapport au Luxe: l'example du Québec", Asac Proceedings, June, pp.13–7.

3   Wong and Ahuvia, 1997, "Personal Taste and Family Face: Luxury Consumption in Confucian and Western Societies", *Psychology and Marketing*.

4   Bond, 1988, "Finding Universal Dimensions of Individual Variation in Multicultural Studies of Values: the Rokeach and Chinese Value Surveys", *Journal of Personality and Social Psychology*, Vol. 55, No. 6, pp.1,009–15; Cheng and Schweitzer, 1996, "Cultural Values Reflected in Chinese and U.S. Television Commercials", *Journal of Advertising Research*, 36 (3), 27–45; Lin, 2001, "Cultural Values Reflected in Chinese and American Television Advertising", *Journal of Advertising*, Winter, Vol. 30, Issue 4.

5   Epstein, S., 1990, "Cognitive-experiential self-theory" in: L.A. Pervin (Ed.), *Handbook of personality: Theory and research*, New York: Guilford Press, pp.165–92.

6   See, for example, Eagly and Chaiken, 1993, *Resistance and Persistence Processes in Attitude Change, The Psychology of Attitudes*, Harcourt Brace Jovanovich College Publishers, pp.559–624.

7   Glenn, 1980, "Values, Attitudes and Beliefs" in O. G. Brim Jr., and K. Kagan (Eds), *Constancy and change in human development* (pp. 596-640), Cambridge: Harvard University Press.

8   Kluckhohn, 1951, "Values and Value Orientations in the Theory of Action" in T. Parsons and E. A. Shils (Eds), *Toward a General Theory of Action*, Cambridge, MA: Harvard University Press.

9   Williams, Robin, 1970, *American Society: A Sociological Interpretation*, New York: Knopf.

10   Hechter, 1993, "Values research in the social and behavioral sciences" in Hechter, M., L. Nadel, and R. E. Michod (Eds), *Sociology and economics: Controversy and integration*, Hawthorne, NY: Aldine de Gruyter.

11   Rokeach, 1973, *The Open and Closed Mind*, Basic Books, New York.

12   Kamakura and Novak, 1992, "Value-system Segmentation: Exploring the Meaning of LOV", *Journal of Consumer Research*.

13   Yang, 1989, "Une conception du Comportement du Consommateur Chinois", *Recherche et Applications en Marketing*, Vol. IV, No. 1, pp17-36.

14   Zhang and Jolibert, 2003, "Les Valeurs Traditionnelles des Acheteurs Chinois: Raffinement Conceptuel, Mesure et Application", *Recherche et Applications en Marketing*, Vol. 18, No. 1.

15   Usunier, 1997, "Consommation ostentatoire et valeurs asiatiques", *Decision Marketing*, No. 10, January–April.

16   "The Southern School of Chinese painting, often called 'literati painting', is a term used to denote art and artists which stand in opposition to the formal Northern School of painting. Where professional, formal painters were classified as Northern School, scholar-bureaucrats who had either retired from the professional world or who were never a part of it constituted the Southern School." Source: answers.com

17   Yang, 1989, op. cit.

18   Zhang and Jolibert, 2003, op. cit.

19   Bond, 1988, op. cit.

20   Chu and Ju, 1993, *The Great Wall in Ruins*, N.Y. State University of New York Press; Hinkelman.

21   Cheng and Schweitzer, op. cit.

22   Lin, op. cit.

23   Yang, 1989, op. cit.; Zhang and Jolibert, 2003.

24   Bond, 1988, op. cit.

25   Eisenstadt, 1973, *Tradition, Change, and Modernity*, New York: John Wiley & Sons, Inc.

26   Chu and Ju, 1993, op. cit.

27   Ibid; Wong and Ahuvia, op. cit.; Lin, op. cit.

28   Bond, 1988, op. cit.

29   Cheng and Schweitzer, 1996, op. cit.

30   Helmut Schütte, 2000, *Consumer Behavior in Asia*, Macmillan.

31   俭,德之共也;侈,恶之大也。—《左传·庄公二十四年》(From Duke Zhuang, 24th year, in « Zuo Zhuan », the first Chinese chronological history, chronicles events during the Spring and Autumn period (770–476 B.C.) of China's history)

32 司马光以亲切的笔调写了《训俭示康》一文，目的在告诫其子司马康要 "以俭素为美"，而不要 "以奢糜为荣"。Si-ma Guang（A．D. 1019–86) of Song Dynasty (A.D. 960–1279).

33 满招损,谦受益。——《书·大禹谟》

34 Weber, M., 1963, *The Religion of China*, New York: Free Press; and 1974, The Protestant Ethic and the Spirit of Capitalism, Unwin University Books, Twelfth Impression.

35 士不可以不弘毅,任重而道远。——《论语· 泰伯》

36 Bond, 1988, cit.

37 Bond, 1988, op. cit.

38 Wong and Ahuvia, 1997, op. cit.

39 Hsu, F.L.K., 1981. "American and Chinese: Passage to differences", Honolulu, HI, University of Hawaii Press; Wong and Ahuvia, 1997, op. cit.

40 Lin, *My country and my people*, William Heinemann, London, 1936; Munro, *Individualism and holism: Studies in Confucian and Taoist values*, Center for Chinese Studies, University of Michigan, 1985; Nisbett et al, 2001, "Culture and system of thought: holistic versus analytic cognition", *Psychological Review*, Vol. 108, No. 2, pp.291–310.

41 Cromer, 1993, *Uncommon sense: The heretical nature of science*, Oxford University Press, New York; Nisbett et al, op. cit.

42 Cui Geng and Liu, Qiming, 2001, "Executive Insights: Emerging Market Segments in a Transitional Economy: A Study of Urban Consumers in China", *Journal of International Marketing*.

43 Cheng and Schweitzer, 1996, op. cit.; Lin, 2001, op. cit.

44 Shimp and Sharma, 1987, "Consumer Ethnocentrism: Construction and Validation of the CETSCALE", *Journal of Marketing Research*.

45 Cheng and Schweitzer, 1996, op. cit.

46 Eisenstadt, 1973, op. cit.

47 Schütte, 2000, op. cit.

48 Belk, Russell, 1985, "Three Scales to Measure Constructs Related to Materialism, Trait Aspects of Living in the Material World", *Journal of Consumer Research*; Netemeyer, Burton and Lichtenstein, 1995, "Trait Aspects of Vanity: Measurement and Relevance to Consumer Behavior", *Journal of Consumer Research*.

49 Tai and Tam, 1996, "A comparative study of Chinese consumers in Asian markets—a lifestyle analysis", *Journal of International Consumer Marketing*; Schütte, 2000, op. cit.

50 Bond, 1988, op. cit.; Cheng and Schweitzer, 1996, op. cit.; Lin, 2001, op. cit.

51   Deng's theory, (1978–97), *Selected works of Deng Xiaoping,* 1998.

52   Mainland and Hong Kong Closer Economic Partnership Arrangement.

53   China opened up outbound tourism in 1990; Singapore, Malaysia, and Thailand were the first countries to get ADS status. Two years later, Japan and Russia joined the list. In 2003, the European Union and China signed a tourism agreement that paved the way for Chinese tour groups to travel to Europe. It extends the ADS status to nearly all EU countries except Britain, Denmark, and Ireland. Countries that Chinese travelers are able to visit with only one visa are: Belgium, Germany, France, Italy, Luxemburg, the Netherlands, Greece, Spain, Portugal, Sweden, Austria, and Finland. Britain and Ireland are expected to soon sign separate ADS Memoranda of Understanding with China. Denmark signed an MOU with China in February 2004. Earlier, Chinese citizens could only travel to the EU on business or family visits.

54   According to the estimation of Organisation mondiale de tourisme (MOT-WTO), 100 million Chinese will travel abroad by 2020 and China is currently ranked fourth—behind Germany, Japan, and the U.S.—in the number of overseas tourists it provides. In 2003, the average spending of Chinese overseas tourists was HK$6,018, as against the average of HK$5,477 for U.S. tourists. In that same year, the British Tourism Organization reported that Chinese Mainlanders in Britain spent more than £127 million.

55   Chu and Ju, op. cit.

56   Cheng and Schweitzer, 1996, op. cit.; Lin, 2001, op. cit.

57   Geert Hofstede, 1991, *Cultures and Organizations,* McGraw-Hill, London.

CHAPTER 4

A Typology of Chinese Luxury Consumers

Things of a kind come together.

People of a mind fall into the same group.

Liu Xiang (Han dynasty, 77–6 B.C.),

Stratagems of the Warring States

S UCH IS the interest in luxury products in China that an article in *The Economist* in June 2004 reported that "The Chinese are replacing the Japanese as the world's most fanatical luxury shoppers."[1] The industry estimates there may be anything up to 100 million Mainland Chinese customers for luxury goods: mostly entrepreneurs and young professionals working for multinational firms, the majority live on the east coast in cities such as Shanghai, Beijing, Dalian, and Shenzhen.

The article presents a general image of Chinese luxury consumers:

> In China, attitudes to luxury have changed dramatically from just a few years ago, when any form of ostentation was frowned upon. Today's Chinese, above all the young, love to flaunt their status. Whereas people in the West are buying more discreetly branded luxury goods identifiable only by those "in the know", the Chinese favor prominent logos that shout, "Look, I'm rich."[2]

While it may be true that the Chinese, like their Asian neighbors, love brands, it is nevertheless a generalization to assume that all Chinese luxury consumers show off and are ostentatious consumers. Some of the more discreet brands—Hermès, Longchamps, and Lancel among them—have enjoyed tremendous success in China as well, while some of the flashier brands—Fendi, Loewe, Givenchy, and Kenzo, for example— are struggling in the market. Conspicuousness is not the only dimension to examine if we are to understand Chinese luxury consumers; their consumption behaviors are not simply attempts to buy class and status, as the media would often have us believe.

Before we examine the alternative ways of looking at this phenomenon, a word about the methodologies used in collecting and collating the results and conclusions reached in this book.

Methodologies

The qualitative study

After reviewing the main questions raised by the literature and the ambivalent attitudes with respect to luxury goods, it was clear that an empirical study was necessary to investigate thoroughly the attitudes and behaviors of luxury goods consumers belonging to the Chinese elite. In-depth interviews were undertaken and the results used to build a tentative model.

Positivism vs. interpretativism

In consumer-research paradigms, two principal approaches have been defined and used by researchers: positivism and interpretativism. Positivism regards the discipline of consumer-behavior studies as an applied marketing science, its main focus being on consumer decision-making. Quantitative studies are positivist methods. The objectives are to be descriptive in nature, enabling marketers to "predict" consumer behavior. Research methods include experiments, survey techniques, and observation. Findings are descriptive, empirical, and generalizable.[3]

Interpretativism, on the other hand, is a postmodernist approach to the study of consumer behavior that focuses on the act of consuming rather than on the act of buying. It focuses on understanding consumption practices, the thinking behind it being that there is no single, objective, truth and that reality is subjective. Cause and effect cannot be isolated; each consumption experience is unique. Interpretativism uses qualitative research, such as in-depth interviews, focus groups, metaphor analysis, collage research, and projective techniques. Researcher/respondent interactions affect research, findings and the findings tend to be subjective.[4]

However, the two research paradigms are complementary in nature and combining qualitative and quantitative research findings produces a richer and more robust profile of consumer behavior than either research approach used alone.[5]

In-depth interview

For this study, in-depth interviews were conducted in two cities of China's most prosperous regions (Beijing in the north and Shanghai in the east), providing rich information and an understanding of what is actually happening in today's China. It is only through the use of these "soft data" that the relationships between different elements can be explored and explained.

The sample size was determined by theoretical saturation, the point at which no more information will enable the theory to be enriched. Clearly, it is impossible to know in advance when this point will be reached and data collection usually ends when the analysis fails to supply any new elements. This principle is based on the law of diminishing returns—the idea that each additional unit of information will supply slightly less new information than the preceding one, until the new information dwindles to nothing.[6]

Gathering data

In the first stage of data collection, 20 interviews were conducted in the chosen geographical locations: 10 in Beijing and Tianjin, representing the northern region, and 10 in Shanghai, representing the east. Beijing and Shanghai are two of the three most dynamic economic and commercial hubs of China.[7] In the second stage, two supplementary interviews were conducted in order to attain saturation.

Details of the 22 interviewees—13 women and nine men—are set out in Table 4.1 below. They ranged in age from 27 to 35, and 18 of these held a master's degree (MBA level). All were senior managers or higher and played a key role in a wide range of business activities: from pharmaceuticals to information technology; from the law to advertising; from fashion and cosmetics to engineering and construction. All earned RMB5,000 or more per year; that is, above the average household income in 2006. From an economic point of view, they are the elite of society.

Each face-to-face interview, lasting between 60 and 90 minutes, was

TABLE 4.1: *Respondent profiles*

No.	Sex	Age	Married	No. of Children	Profession	Title
1	F	36	Yes	1	Pharmaceuticals	Director
2	F	29	Yes	1	IT	Engineer
3	F	31	No	0	Consulting	Director
4	F	33	Yes	1	Law	Legal Manager
5	M	30	No	0	Advertising	VP
6	M	33	Yes	0	IT	Solution Alliance Consultant
7	M	34	Yes	0	Engineering	Business Development Engineer
8	M	36	Yes	0	Investment	Assistant General Manager
9	M	42	Yes	1	IT	Deputy General Manager
10	F	29	Yes	1	Transportation	Director for Export Business
11	F	33	No	0	Telecommunication	Chief Business Planning Officer
12	F	31	Yes	1	Cosmetics	Brand Manager
13	F	31	Yes	1	Cosmetics	Assistant to President
14	M	29	No	0	Foods	Product Manager
15	F	33	Yes	1	Pharmaceuticals	Manager
16	M	34	Yes	1	Construction	President
17	M	37	Yes	1	Insurance	Director
18	F	37	Yes	1	Publishing	Project Manager
19	F	26	No	0	Fashion	Designer
20	F	32	Yes	1	Distribution	IT Director
21*	F	34	No	0	Energy	Human Resources Director
22*	M	35	Yes	0	Construction	VP of Purchasing

* Supplemental interviews. The profiles of respondents were updated in 2007.

digitally recorded, transcribed, and translated from Chinese to English by professional translators, and double-checked by experts.

The questionnaire consisted of two parts. The first focused on general luxury consumption and the respondents' attitudes toward luxury goods, the notions of luxury, and luxury consumption. The questions, all open-ended, included "Can you remember and describe your latest purchase of luxury products?" and "What does luxury mean to you?" The second part focused on discussions about cultural values, consumption values, some social changes, and social topics such as: "What do you think about

Education level	City	Region	Income Scale (RMB)	Car	Apartment
MBA	Tianjin	North	20,000–25,000	Yes	Yes
Bachelor	Beijing	North	15,000–20,000	Yes	Yes
MBA	Beijing	North	20,000–25,000	Yes	Yes
MBA	Beijing	North	25,000–30,000	Yes	Yes
Bachelor	Beijing	North	30,000–35,000	Yes	Yes
MBA	Beijing	North	15,000–20,000	Yes	Yes
MBA	Beijing	North	15,000	Yes	Yes
MBA	Beijing	North	20,000– 25,000	Yes	Yes
MBA	Beijing	North	30,000–35,000	Yes	Yes
Bachelor	Beijing	North	15,000–20,000	Yes	Yes
Master	Shanghai	East	20,000–25,000	Yes	Yes
Master	Shanghai	East	15,000–20,000	Yes	Yes
MBA	Shanghai	East	15,000	Yes	Yes
Master	Shanghai	East	15,000–20,000	Yes	Yes
MBA	Shanghai	East	15,000–20,000	Yes	Yes
MBA	Shanghai	East	above 50,000	Yes	Yes
MBA	Shanghai	East	20,000–25,000	No	Yes
MBA	Shanghai	East	15,000	No	Yes
MBA	Shanghai	East	15,000	No	Yes
MBA	Shanghai	East	15,000	No	Yes
Master	Beijing	North	25,000–30,000	No	Yes
Master	Beijing	North	15,000–20,000	Yes	Yes

Chinese traditional values, such as frugality, in your life?" and "Do you think to be wealthy is a glorious thing?"

The interviews and observation data were analyzed by thematic content, with great care taken to avoid as much as possible the researcher's subjective bias in the qualitative study.

The quantitative study

The qualitative research identified three types of psychographic variables—consumer information process, consumer values, meaning of luxury products—which were then used as the basis for a segmentation of the luxury consumer market into four categories—Lovers, Intellectuals, Followers, and Laggards—based on a sample of 351 consumers. Then, we looked at the differences in luxury buying characteristics—Innovativeness, Brand Loyalty, and Post-Purchase Guilt—between the classified groups and the direct relationships between the psychographic variables and the post-purchase characteristics.

The data were collected over a period of two months in 2004, via both the Internet and by direct contact in the main economic hubs. The final sample data of 315 observations comprised 214 women (67.9 %) and 101 men (32.1%).

All main economic hubs of the mainland—that is, Beijing in the North (147, 46.7%), Shanghai in the East (92, 29.2%), Guangdong in the South (40, 12.7%), Chengdu in the Center and West (30, 9.5%), and Hong Kong, Macao, Taiwan, and Overseas Chinese (6, 1.9%)—were included, reflecting the respective economic weights of each mainland region and the luxury industry distributions in the market.

More than 90% of the respondents were 21 to 35 years old, an age range that corresponds very well with the targeted consumer segment—the elite. Some 90% of respondents earned more than 5,000 RMB per month[8] (five times the average monthly salary in mainland China cities), meaning they qualify for the middle and upper-middle class designations very early in their professional careers and have the financial wherewithal to purchase luxury products. Some 5.5% of the total sample earned more than RMB15,000 per month.

As to the level of education achieved, 65.1% held a bachelor's degree, 22.5% held a master's, and 1% had doctorates. Of the remainder, 1.4% had only high-school level qualifications and another 10% had had professional or technical training.

The sample represented a diverse range of business activities, the vast majority (more than 93%) being office-based professionals—clerks, managers, senior managers, and CEOs—drawn from 20 professional categories including advertising/marketing/PR, finance/insurance/real-estate services, computers/electronics, telecommunications, retail, and consumer goods. Other occupations recorded included artists and independent workers/professionals.

The luxury consumption of China's elite

Previous studies had raised a number of issues that had to be taken into consideration:

Brand awareness, brand loyalty, and the domestic market

Some studies of European luxury consumption had found that brand awareness was no longer considered necessary.[9] In Europe, luxury consumption has become more discreet and pays more attention to personal involvement than to the more conspicuous social aspects of luxury purchases. However, in Asian countries, brand awareness and luxury products are inextricably linked in consumers' minds. In the Asian market, a brand may have all the accepted attributes of a luxury product but, without brand awareness, it will be considered as a high-quality product or a work of art, rather than as a real luxury brand.

In another study, brand awareness is the ability of a potential buyer to recognize or recall that a brand is a member of a certain product category: a link between product class and brand is involved.[10] For luxury brands and products, brand awareness is the most important element for some luxury consumers in China, as these extracts from our research interviews clearly illustrate:

> "Anyway, I feel that the good reputation can make me feel secure when I purchase. I am a person who is easily influenced by advertising. I will believe in the company or brand who can convince me. Once I feel what you say is true, I will buy your product. For example, a car costing two million yuan, maybe it is an unknown brand, maybe it is a very famous brand but unknown to me, I will not pay much attention to that. Of course, if it is a BMW, I will look at it more than others. Because I feel it is a good car, I feel it from my heart that it is a good car. It is a kind of feeling."

> "If the price is high, the quality should be very good, the company should be prestigious, internationally famous, and the brand preferable in the eyes of most people in the high income class."

Brand awareness in the domestic market is a necessity, because of the higher price and conspicuous function of the products. Consumers choose only from among famous brands and are not willing to risk spending large sums of money on the unknown, even if the unknown is a prestigious brand internationally, as the following comments reveal:

> "[I]f I don't know the brand, I will not buy it ... all my friends are like me."

> "[I]f nobody knows the brand here [in the domestic market], I would never buy it, even if it is very famous abroad."

> "I asked my brother in the U.S. to buy Clinique for me. But he said that it was a very common brand and could be found in

supermarkets everywhere. He told me which was the most internationally famous brand and suggested that I buy a gift package to try. But I had never heard about that brand here. So I told him not to buy it. I prefer the brand that I know and have heard about here."

Brand loyalty and brand attachment

Brand loyalty is a measure of the attachment that a consumer has to a brand[11] and this can arise from a range of reasons and motivations. For Chinese consumers, the function and image based on understanding the brand plays a strong role in establishing loyalty toward a brand and its product range, as illustrated in the following respondent's comments:

"I just bought a bag from Lancel: a very ordinary model, very classical. And I have a back-bag from Lancel too … [T]he quality and the style tell people that it is a Lancel. If you know and use Lancel, you will recognize it immediately. I really love it. I just feel that it is modest, simple. It is the same for Lancel's suitcase. I would have bought one, but I couldn't because I had too much baggage. [I] will continue to try its products in other categories. My wallet is also a Lancel, my key bag too."

For the following respondent, loyalty to the brand is based on its functions and services. It is also an example of the success of a domestic brand with a Western name, which is now considered to be a European brand in the Chinese luxury market:

"I wear only certain brands. For example, Caristo, an Italian brand … Why do I like this brand? You know, for us, the Latin languages; words finishing with a vowel are very nice to hear. Secondly, their color matches my personality; very soft and smooth, not ostentatious at all. Finally, the service is excellent …"

Personal involvement, dream, vanity, and conspicuousness

Personal involvement and happiness of possession

Involvement is distinguished by pleasure and the semiotic and symbolic values of luxury brands; happiness of possession is linked with the extended self and identification.[12] The two elements are found to co-exist in an individual's consumption behavior. For example, for the following respondents, luxury products fulfill their dreams and give them the happiness of possession. They also bring the happiness of being seen as a member of particular group.

> "I was very happy about that. I really love them. I wear [the ring] now to remind me of my first salary and my independence."

> "It is to fulfill my desire to be pretty, everyone loves beautiful things … Anyway, at that time, all the pretty girls wore this model of ring, so I made my mind up that I had to buy one."

> "I was very excited and delighted with the bracelet. I feel it was a good bargain. Because we say that jade is priceless. And my bracelet is made of both emerald and jade. So, in terms of quality, it is an 'A' grade jade from Burma."

Dream value

For the Chinese elite, the dream value of a luxury product is its ability to make an individual dream of possessing it and, once it is possessed, enjoy the satisfaction of saying "the dream has come true." In Western countries, this dream value is mostly associated with elitist culture.[13]

As we saw earlier, Asian consumers appreciate the legendary models of luxury brands and limited collections and, because of the dream value, Chinese elite consumers are ready to pay much more for luxury products:

> "The happy few rich people can buy luxury products all the time if they like; but ordinary people like me buy luxury products for a particular reason … when you get married or get a promotion. It is a gift for yourself … For rich people, luxury products are symbols of social class; for ordinary people, luxury products may be a dream or have sentimental value."

> "It is just to fulfill one of my dreams of something I have wanted for a very long time. I didn't have lots of money, as my salary was low as a newly graduated university student, but to fulfill my desire, I saved several months' salary to buy the luxury products that I had longed for for many years."

A product's reputation and the desire to fulfill personal dreams are key drivers for Chinese consumers to buy luxury goods, and a trip, whether for business or pleasure, is a good occasion for luxury buying:

> "My first luxury product was a jade bracelet. I bought it when I was in Kun Ming[14] during one of my business trips. I spent 2000 yuan, which at that time represented a huge amount. Jade from Burma has a very high reputation."

Vanity and conspicuousness

Conspicuous consumption has been shown to be linked with vanity—both physical vanity and that which comes from achievement.[15] The latter is easily observable in the Chinese elite group, especially for products considered to be symbols of success. For example, a private car is seen as an important indicator of success in business. The brand and the specific model of the car indicate the wealth of the owner:

> "[A] car is very important for me. All my female colleagues in the sales and marketing departments have a car. [They] all drive to

the office every morning. When we meet or accompany clients, driving a car means that your work performance has arrived at a certain level which allows you to have a private car. That is the effect on clients. In addition, I feel proud of myself in front of my colleagues… Of course, the car I drive must be better than theirs; if it was inferior to theirs, it would be worse than nothing."

"For everything that we can see and can be seen, I choose luxury brands and products; for example, a watch and a car. The car is more important, because you will drive the car yourself and it will be seen by everybody."

Word of mouth, imitation, and the pursuit of fashion

Word of mouth

Recent studies have suggested that word of mouth influences product consumption and brand choice. This is also evident in the behavior of Chinese elite consumers. Comments and recommendations from friends and colleagues play an important, sometimes decisive, role in brand and product choice.

"I accept the opinions of friends, especially girls, [who say they] have tried something which is very good."

"…the guide, a woman from Hong Kong, influenced me very much. She told me that she had [bought] some diamonds and that all the money she earned was spent on diamonds. I was strongly influenced by her."

And the comments and recommendations from virtual communities on the Internet serve the same function, perhaps even stronger:

> "I went to some [Web sites] to see other users' comments about different brands and products. People like to put their comments on the chat room and discuss with others ... Lancôme has lots of products, but the recommendation says that the night cream is the best. So I bought it."

Brand choices are definitely influenced by word of mouth and by the image, quality, and long history of the brand:

> "I always choose Longines. I think Longines women's watches are really very nice. For example, my model, this one is super thin, very popular. Rolex women's watches are not very big either, but my colleagues all consider that the Longines super-thin model is the best."

For some people, brand history is an absolute necessity in a luxury brand;

> "... it must have some historical background; it takes a very long time to build that up."

For others, it is unimportant:

> "I don't care about that so much, I don't care about the origin of the brand, which country it comes from."

Attitudes differ according to product category. For example, for watches and jewelry, the history of the product is an important part of their reputation. Consumers accept history as a key indicator for a prestige watch or jewelry brand:

> "If the quality is good, maybe they can be kept for a hundred years. So I feel these things are quite different, they have value."

"For me the long history of the brand is important. I like the feeling that it's a brand with a history."

"My dream brand, of course, is Rolex. I have a friend from the U.S. who wears a 100-year-old Rolex. I feel that it is very valuable."

Imitation and the pursuit of fashion

Imitation can lead to an individual becoming identified as a member of a certain group, with particular tastes and social standing:

"And at that time, this kind of ring was very popular; all the pretty girls wore this model, so I decided that I must buy one."

"If my colleagues use it and everybody uses it, I will buy it and try it."

"Recently, everybody is rushing to buy Lancôme. When I was in France, Guerlain and Givenchy were more expensive than Lancôme. When I told my friends in China, they didn't believe me. They said that it was impossible; they'd heard that Lancôme is the best in France and in the world. This shows that L'Oréal's marketing work in China is really well done!"

Western influence on luxury consumption

Since the opening of China in 1978, young people—both urban and rural—have been increasingly exposed to foreign products and services. Many of the Chinese elite have had overseas experience, whether in their studies, their professions, or their leisure activities. This, and their experience of luxury consumption abroad, has had a profound influence on their way of thinking and on their own purchasing behavior. Economic development and frequent international exchange have led to greater acceptance of Western products in the domestic market. This too was revealed in the comments in response to a question on whether their European experiences had influenced their behavior as consumers:

> "I am sure that my foreign experience has had an important influence on my lifestyle and my consumption choices ... brand choices, product choices, such as the baguette in France. Before I went to France, I never wanted to eat and buy a baguette in China. But after my stay in Paris, I could accept it, because I had tried it and felt that it was good, including cheese. I think it has a very strong influence on me; at least you know many more European brands which are certainly not very famous here. When you come back, when you see the same things, the first feeling in your mind is 'I know this one.' I think the lifestyle also has influences on what you eat and what you wear, because you have already had some experience of these brands and products."

Personal choice in different product categories

An individual's luxury consumption behavior cannot be generalized across all categories, because luxury buying and consumption are directly linked with personal tastes and an understanding of the social functions of luxury products. For example, an individual who buys only luxury brands in cosmetics and perfumes may never buy a luxury table decoration or writing instrument.

Consumption priorities vary according to the gender of consumers. For men, luxury consumption tends to be focused on watches and cars, as symbols of achievement, success, and social status. Women, on the other hand, are more focused on clothing and cosmetics.

Pricing

Price is still a key factor for Chinese luxury consumers. Although a higher price is a key element of luxury goods, there is still a strong instinctive impulse to bargain, whether the product is a luxury watch or a kilo of tomatoes. It depends on where the product is bought: domestically or abroad, online or in a shopping center.

Chinese luxury consumers buy most of their products abroad during business trips or holidays, or ask friends and relatives abroad to bring back the luxury articles they want. The fundamental reason for this is that prices are much lower abroad, as the following comments reveal:

> "It will be cheaper by at least a half in Hong Kong than here in Beijing."

> "My wife is a tourist guide; she goes to Hong Kong regularly. It is she who brings the brands we need from there."

> "Even if the price and models are the same, I think people prefer to spend money abroad; maybe they think expensive things should be bought abroad."

Much depends, too, on the availability of goods of the required quality at home:

> "For shoes, it is surely much more expensive than in the domestic market, but I prefer to buy them here [in Paris], because obviously the design and quality are much better."

The role of Internet buying

Because of the simplicity, rapidity, and lower price offers, online purchasing has been adopted by the Chinese elite and is becoming one of their major purchasing channels for cosmetics and perfumes. The explanations given for this by our respondents included:

"Because this is a very big Web site, it can guarantee that the products sold are genuine. And it is one-third cheaper than in domestic department stores."

"It is handy and has free delivery service. I pay when the product arrives. Generally, the price is one-third cheaper than in shopping centers."

"The brand has to pay shopping center location rent, personal fees, and logistic fees etc. That is why the price is higher than that of online stores. But for online stores, the costs are really very low …"

In addition to the lower prices, the convenience offered by the Internet is beginning to affect the way people go about their luxury shopping. As one respondent said:

"The products are classified by category. You choose what you want, and they are delivered the next day. Once the delivery arrives, you pay for the products … So I don't go to shopping centers to buy cosmetics any more. The pre-condition is that I know the product very well [beforehand]."

For other luxury categories, online purchasing is less popular. Some products need to be examined, compared, and tried out at the selling point. This is certainly the case for fashion brands. For luxury jewelry and watches, too, every piece is unique and needs to be carefully examined before a decision can be made. What the consumer experiences during the purchasing process is an important part of luxury consumption. A virtual visit online is unable to respond to such demands on the part of prospective consumers.

To summarize: there are three important attributes that define a luxury brand in China: high brand awareness, high price, and excellent quality. The dream value, long history of the brand, and uniqueness of the product are supplementary attributes about which attitudes vary.

Psychographic traits, consumer process, and the meaning of luxury products

Demographic and psychographic variables can be used as a basis for segmentation.

The psychographic segmentation method divides consumers into different groups on the basis of lifestyle, personality, and values.[16] The opposing values and different information processes that emerged in our findings allow us to use the psychographic approach to study the Chinese elite market.

Psychological values

The first group of variables is consumer values. As described and discussed earlier, it consists of two groups of opposing values in luxury consumption: collectivism and individualism. In China, collectivism has long been the accepted social ethic, in both Confucian tradition and under Communism since 1949. Personal freedom and individualism are emerging under Western cultural influences and through international exchange. Individualism is becoming much more of an influence on the younger generation. A commonly held view of these changes is captured in the following comments from one of our respondents:

> "Western countries are more developed than us and their lifestyles can easily attract young people, [through] values such as openness, liberty, freedom, as shown in American films. In fact, on the basis of more developed materialistic cultures, our young people think that everything is better in Western countries, including, art, cinema, and all these cultural aspects."

Chinese luxury consumers are finding ways to combine these opposing elements in their consumption behavior, as the following illustrates:

"I think the teaching of frugality is not inconsistent with the teaching of values such as autonomy and independence. Of course, I don't demand of my parents that they support the luxury life that I like. If I want to have this kind of life, I have to support myself. If I earn 1 million and spend 999,000, nobody can say anything, because it is I who earned the money. So I will teach the value of independence to my children. If they always compare the products they use with others, and always demand that their parents buy them, this isn't acceptable and isn't a good habit."

The consumer process

Personality influences the attitude of consumers. Some individuals are easily influenced by advertising and the opinions of others. They have impulsive and compulsive characteristics; others are more analytical and do not easily change their mind.[17]

Studies in psychology have identified two fundamentally different modes of processing information: one is intuitive, automatic, imagistic/non-verbal, and experiential; the other is more analytical, rational, verbal, and deliberative.[18] The implications of this for luxury consumption behaviors are important.

As Epstein indicated, analytical thinking in the rational system and impulsive thinking in the experiential system create an attitudinal ambivalence, as evidenced in the dissonance and guilt felt by the following respondent when she subjects her impulsive buying to post-purchase analysis:

"I think that I am a person who has a rule to follow and can restrain myself. My budget is always under control. What I buy is not very extravagant. However, sometimes I see clothes that I really love and buy them, even though I have lots of similar things already. When I get home, I feel very guilty, thinking that I wasted money again."

Conspicuous vs. functional

The meaning of luxury products in the Chinese cultural context is another important aspect of luxury consumption. For some people, conspicuousness and high brand awareness are important; for others, functionality and quality are the key elements behind their decisions to choose certain luxury products.

Propositions of segmentation

As we have seen, there are a number of pairs of opposing values at work in the minds of Chinese luxury consumers: the individualism of the new ideology (modernity, wealth, success/achievement) versus the collectivism of Chinese tradition (frugality, economy, modesty/humility); the impulsive and experiential versus the analytical and rational; and the conspicuous social aspect versus the functional individual aspect.

Psychographic segmentation

In a psychographic segmentation—which is linked to lifestyle analysis—consumers are divided into different groups on the basis of their lifestyle, attitudes, personalities, and values. People within the same demographic group can exhibit very different psychographic profiles.[19] This form of applied consumer research has proven to be a valuable marketing tool that helps identify consumer segments that are likely to be responsive to specific marketing messages.[20] Because psychographic characteristics provide a rich view of the market and a more lifelike portrait of the consumer, they meet the demands of management practice for increasingly sophisticated and actionable marketing information.[21]

As previous qualitative research has shown, several demographic criteria can be used to define the Chinese elite,[22] who belong to one social group with similar demographic characteristics: city-dwellers with high levels of education, high-level occupations, and high incomes.

Based on the in-depth interviews, we identified three dimensions as the basis of our consumer segmentation: consumer process (a personality-linked dimension comprising two opposing variables: impulsive and analytical); consumer values (comprising four variables: modernity, success/wealth, frugality/modesty, and collectivism/interdependence or individualism/personal freedom); and the meaning of luxury products in a Chinese cultural background.

On the basis of these three dimensions, the four segments that emerged were classified as Luxury Lovers, Luxury Followers, Luxury Intellectuals, and Luxury Laggards, as shown in Figures 4.1, 4.2, and 4.3. (These classifications are explained in more detail in the segment profiles below.)

FIGURE 4.1: *Consumer values/Meaning of luxury*

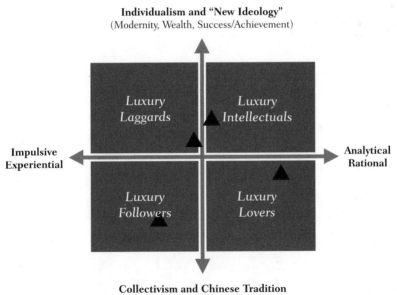

Individualism and "New Ideology"
(Modernity, Wealth, Success/Achievement)

Luxury Laggards

Luxury Intellectuals

Impulsive Experiential

Analytical Rational

Luxury Followers

Luxury Lovers

Collectivism and Chinese Tradition
Frugality, Economy, and Modesty

FIGURE 4.2: *Consumer values/Meaning of luxury*

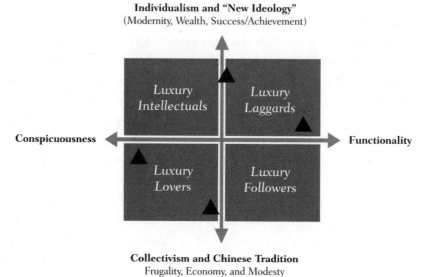

Individualism and "New Ideology"
(Modernity, Wealth, Success/Achievement)

Conspicuousness ← → Functionality

Luxury Intellectuals

Luxury Laggards

Luxury Lovers

Luxury Followers

Collectivism and Chinese Tradition
Frugality, Economy, and Modesty

FIGURE 4.3: *Consumer information process/Meaning of luxury dimension*

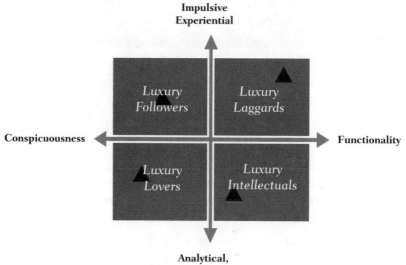

Impulsive Experiential

Conspicuousness ← → Functionality

Luxury Followers

Luxury Laggards

Luxury Lovers

Luxury Intellectuals

Analytical, Rational

The four groups of consumers were classified with the three factors through a hierarchical cluster analysis,[23] the results of which are summarized in Table 4.1.

TABLE 4.1: *Results of Psychographic Segmentation Analysis*

Chinese Luxury Consumer Market Segmentation	Factor 1: Individualist	Factor 2: Conspicuous	Factor 3: Impulsive	Frequency (315)	Percent %
Lovers	–	++	–	48	15.2
Followers	– –	+	+	69	21.9
Intellectuals	++	–	–	111	35.2
Laggards	+	– –	+	87	27.6

+ indicates individuals are mainly situated on the positive side of the factor
– means individuals are mainly situated on the negative side of the factor

Segment profiles

Segment 1: These are the *luxury lovers* (so called because they know exactly what they want as luxury brands and products, love luxury brands, and enjoy the conspicuousness of luxury), of whom there are 48, representing 15.2% of the total. In the consumer-value factor, they are very oriented toward the conspicuous and are rational rather than impulsive.

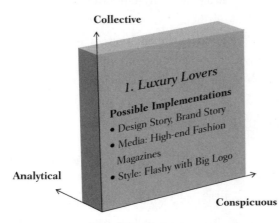

Measured against the individualist factor, they are quite widely dispersed, signifying that this factor alone cannot clearly distinguish members in this segment. In other words, the lovers are not homogeneous. They may be collectivist as well as individualist. Not surprisingly, since luxury lovers are rational and well informed for many product categories and impulsive for others, they are very conspicuously oriented, as expected.

In demographic terms, 60% of the members in this segment are women. The members of this segment are centralized within two age groups: 26–30 and 31–35. Guangzhou (with 22.5%) has more luxury lovers than Beijing (15.6%), Shanghai (13.0%), and Chengdu (3.3%). The income distribution in this segment is situated at the higher income levels, RMB 10,000–14,999 and RMB15,000–19,999 per month. Their jobs are very diverse: office clerks, managers, and senior managers are all possible luxury lovers. In other words, occupation is not a salient characteristic for the profile of this segment. All hold either bachelor's or master's degrees.

Segment 2: The members of this segment, the *luxury followers* (so called because their luxury choices follow the trends created by the media, brands, and public, rather than being based on their own feelings and understanding of luxury products and specific brands), are clearly distinguished by three factors: they are collectivist, very conspicuous, and

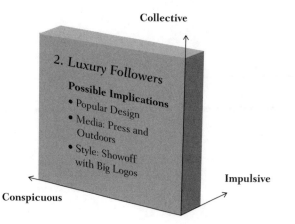

very impulsive. The 69 individuals in this segment represent 21.9% of the sample. All their characteristics are as expected.

The age range of this segment, most of whom are women (72%) is mostly centralized in the 21–25 and 36–40 groups. Chengdu (33%) has the most followers, followed by Guangzhou (27.5%), Shanghai (26.1%), and Beijing (15.6%). Incomes vary widely, from RMB0–4,999 to, at the highest level, RMB15,000–19,999. The numbers on each income level are roughly similar. Most followers are office clerks (52%) and managers (30%), with very few senior managers and CEOs (10%). The vast majority of followers are degree-holders (70% bachelor's and 20% master's).

Segment 3: The *luxury intellectuals* (who have their own understanding of luxury, keep a distance from trends, and prefer discreet, classical models)—the largest of the four groups, with 111 individuals or 35.2% of the total—are very individualistic, not very conspicuous in their consumption, and rational.

Their characteristics are, as expected, in the functional and rational perspective. From the qualitative study they emerged as being individualist but with a slight leaning toward the collective; that is, reliant on friends and family. In the quantitative research, the modern individualist factor confirmed the individualist orientation of the luxury intellectuals.

In gender terms, this is the most well-balanced of the four segments,

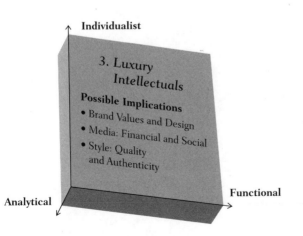

with 55% women. The age ranges are centralized from 21–25 to 31–35. Beijing (with 42.2%) has the most intellectuals, followed by Shanghai (33.7%), Guangzhou (30%), and Chengdu (16.7%). The intellectuals range from office clerks to CEOs and this is reflected perhaps in income levels which vary from RMB0–4,999 to RMB30,000-plus. There is also a considerable variation in education levels.

Segment 4: In general terms, the *luxury laggards* (so called because, although they can afford luxury products, they don't care about luxury brands and are not influenced by advertising) are heterogeneous with regard to the individualist factor and thus functional and rather impulsive. This corresponds to our expectation that they are price-rational but opportunistic buyers, and therefore impulsive. There are 87 individuals classified in this segment, representing 27.6% of the total sample population.

The majority of luxury laggards are women (84%). The age range distribution is very similar to that of the lovers: centralized from 21–25 to 31–35. Chengdu (46.7%) has the most laggards, followed by Beijing (26.5%), Shanghai (27.2%), and Guangzhou (20%). While laggards are present in each income level, most fall into middle level (RMB8,000–9,999). The majority of laggards are office clerks (60%), 30% of them being managers, generally holding a bachelor's degree.

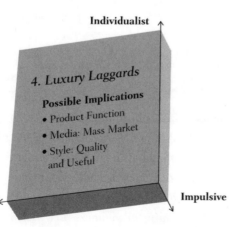

Similar to the lovers, the laggards are dispersed in terms of individualism. Their group centers are near to zero (the lovers with a negative value and the laggards with a positive value). The other two factors, the conspicuousness factor and the impulsive factor, distinguish the luxury laggards and luxury lovers very clearly from the other segments. The results of the qualitative research show that, as expected, the lovers are analytical and not impulsive, while the laggards are more impulsive than rational.

The behavior differences of the four classified groups are analyzed below.

Summary of segment profiles

In examining differences between the four groups we found that two significant correlations played the major roles: individualism and impulsiveness; conspicuousness and innovativeness.

The first correlation indicated that while luxury lovers are rational and collective, luxury laggards are impulsive and individualist in their consumption of luxury goods. For luxury lovers, rational choice is influenced by collective considerations: will this luxury brand/product be recognized by the people I want to impress? For luxury laggards, there are few collective considerations influencing their luxury consumption. Personal preference dictates their choices: if a product has excellent quality and fits their functional needs, they will buy it without too much analysis of social usage.

With regard to the second correlation, between conspicuousness and innovativeness, our findings showed luxury lovers and luxury followers are oriented toward conspicuous consumption behavior, which finds expression in their liking for new trends, new collections, and fashion seasons. Luxury intellectuals and luxury laggards are less conspicuous, and thus their interest in luxury goods lies not in newness but in other elements, such as brand heritage for intellectuals and super quality for laggards.

Based on the two correlations, the second proposed matrix can be adjusted as follows:

FIGURE 4.4: *The adjusted segmentation matrix: individualist/conspicuous*

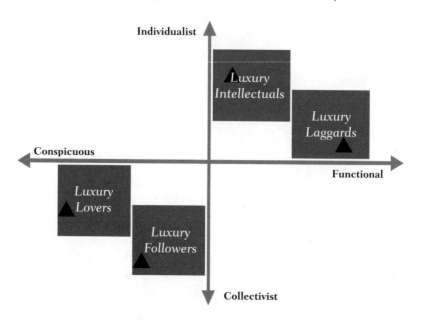

Conspicuousness is linked with the social awareness of the individual; for example, buying conspicuous luxury goods as a display of wealth and success for others. Thus, conspicuous consumers are collectivist too.

There are few functional collectivists among Chinese luxury consumers, who choose specific luxury goods in order to fulfill their functional needs, such as the very act of possession. They are functional individualists and tend to ignore the conspicuousness of the product and focus on excellent quality and sophisticated design. Given a choice between a Rolex and a Breguet, they would ignore the flashy conspicuousness of the former in favor of the quieter, more sophisticated pleasures that owning the latter brings.

A more detailed technical explanation of the analysis can be found in the Appendix.

ENDNOTES

1 "Conspicuous Consumption in China, Luxury's New Empire", *The Economist*, 19th June 2004, p.65.

2 Ibid.

3 Lincoln and Guba, 1985, *Naturalistic Inquiry*, Beverley Hills, CA, Sage.

4 Shiffman and Kanuk, 2001, *Consumer Behavior*, Seventh Edition, Prentice-Hall, Inc., New Jersey.

5 Evard, Pras and Roux, 2003, *Market, Etudes et Recherches en Marketing*, 3e Edition, Dunod, Paris.

6 Thietart et al., 2000, *Doing Management Research*, Sage Publication, London.

7 The third economic and commercial hub is the Guangzhou-Shenzhen-Hong Kong-Macao Region (the Zhujiang Delta) in the South of China.

8 According to UN figures in 2004, the international criterion for middle-class income is US$6,000 per capita per year (RMB5,000 per capita per month). In China, the middle-class annual family income standard is from US$7,264 to US$60,532 (from RMB60,000 to RMB 500,000 per year per family) (2005, National Bureau of Statistics, Beijing).

9 Roux, 1991, "Comment se positionnement les marques de luxe", *Revue Française du Marketing*, No 132-133; Dubois and Duquesne, 1993, "The market for luxury goods : income versus culture", *European Journal of Marketing*, Vol. 27, No 1, pp.35–44; Dubois, Laurent and Czellar, 2000, "Consumer Rapport to Luxury : Analyzing Complex and Ambivalent Attitudes", working paper HEC.

10 Aaker, D., 1991, *Managing Brand Equity*, New York, The Free Press.

11 Ibid.

12 Belk, 2001, "Possessions and the Extended Self", *Journal of Consumer Research*, September.

13 Lipovetsky and Roux, 2003, *Le Luxe Eternel*, Edition Gallimard; Nyeck and Roux, 2003, "Does product category influence in marketing luxury brands" via WWW, Hawaii conference on business, Honolulu, 14th–17th June.

14 Kun Ming is the capital of Yun Nan province in the south of China, near Burma.

15 Netemeyer, Burton and Lichtenstein, 1995, "Traits Aspects of Vanity: Measurement and Relevance to Consumer Behavior", *Journal of Consumer Research*, March.

16 Kotler, 2000, *Marketing Management*, The Millennium Edition, Prentice-Hall, Inc., New Jersey.

17 Faber and O'Guinn, 1992, "A Clinical Screener for Compulsive Buying", *Journal of Consumer Research*, December; Cole and Sherrell, 1995, "Comparing Scales to Measure Compulsive Buying: An Exploration of Their Dimensionality", *Advances in Consumer Research*, Vol. 22.

18 Epstein et al., 1996, "Individual Differences in Intuitive-Experiential and Analytical-Rational Thinking Styles", *Journal of Personality and Social Psychology*, 71(2), pp.390–405.

19 Kotler, op. cit.; Darpy and Volle, 2003, *Comportements du Consommateur: Concepts et Outils*, Paris, Dunod.

20 Schiffman and Kanuk, op. cit.

21 Kamakura and Wedel, 1995, "Lifestyle Segmentation with Tailored Interviewing", *Journal of Marketing Research*, No. 3, August; Oates, Shufeldt and Vaught, 1996, "A Psychographic Study of the Elderly and Retail Store Attributes", *Journal of Consumer Marketing*, Vol. 13, No. 6.

22 Lu, "Consumption and Ambivalent Attitudes of Chinese Young Elite towards Occidental Luxury Goods", 2004, AMA Winter Educators Conference Proceedings, Phoenix.

23 The median clustering method was used in order to divide consumers into homogeneous groups in terms of their psychographic traits. The Pearson correlation was used for Distances Similarity Measures for Interval Data in the median clustering method. The Pearson correlation is the product-moment correlation between two vectors of values. This is the default similarity measure for interval data. The scatter plots were given by projecting the individuals into two or three dimensions with the axes (factors to classify the groups). Both 3D and 2D graphs were obtained. The visualization of the four classified groups in the graphs with the factors facilitates the evaluation work of group profiles. Together with the demographic information of each segment, the profile of segments can be clearly described.

CHAPTER 5

Habits, Lifestyles, Locations

How can you govern a country with 246 varieties of cheese?

Charles de Gaulle (1890–1970)

I N **CHAPTER** 4, we identified four segments of Chinese luxury consumers: luxury lovers, luxury followers, luxury intellectuals, and luxury laggards. Here, we focus on their habits, their lifestyles, and geographic differences.

Three indicators (innovativeness, brand loyalty, and post-purchase guilt) were chosen to examine the attitudinal behavior differences of each group and the study found that the psychographic groups differ significantly in all three indicators.

Product innovations and new trends

In the fashion industry, the two seasons (Spring/Summer and Fall/Winter) of every year are the most important periods. During the respective fashion weeks, talented designers show their new collections to the public and media. It is through these new collections that the following year's luxury fashion trends are transferred all over the world; from Paris to Tokyo; from Milan to Hong Kong; and from New York to Singapore.

In studying consumer behavior, to measure the rapidity of the adoption of innovations, we use the concept of sensibility to innovativeness.

Consumer researchers have endeavored to develop measurement instruments to gauge the level of consumer innovativeness,[1] how quickly consumers adopt these new trends, and ideas created by the most powerful and prestigious fashion houses. Innovativeness is usually taken as a personality trait which provides important insights into the nature and boundaries of a consumer's willingness or tendency to innovate. In this book, however, innovativeness is defined and measured as the attitude toward luxury goods innovations and the new trends of each season.

According to the propositions of Chinese luxury consumer typology, luxury lovers have the most favorable attitudes toward innovation; luxury laggards are the least sensitive to innovations and are the slowest to react (see Figure 5.1).

FIGURE 5.1: *Attitudes to innovation*

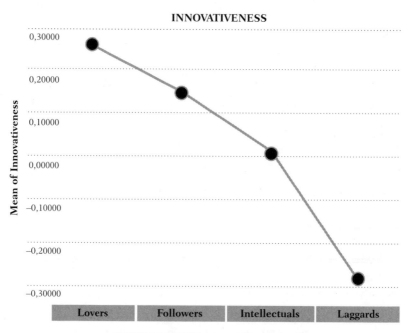

INNOVATIVENESS

CHINESE LUXURY CONSUMER MARKET

In previous marketing research, innovativeness is particularly relevant to technological products (such as home electronics), where some models offer an abundance of features and functions, while others propose just a minimum of essential features or functions.[2] In this study, the results show that for luxury products, the consumer's innovativeness is also an important indicator of the diversity of luxury consumer behavior.

According to Schütte[3] and the traditional diffusion theory, consumers are categorized in relation to when they adopt a new product. The five adopter categories most frequently cited are: innovators, early adopters, early majority, late majority, and laggards. As shown in Figure 5.2, in a Western context, these categories are generally depicted as a normal distribution curve with innovators, early adopters, and laggards accounting for 2.5%, 13.5%, and 16%, respectively,[4] and very specific strategies should be designed for each category.[5]

FIGURE 5.2: *Time of adoption of innovations*

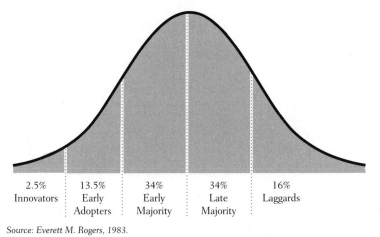

| 2.5% | 13.5% | 34% | 34% | 16% |
| Innovators | Early Adopters | Early Majority | Late Majority | Laggards |

Source: Everett M. Rogers, 1983.

The early and late majorities each account for 34% of the total population which ultimately adopts a product. However, in an Asian cultural context, very few consumers are prepared to take the social risk of being the first to try a new product. The discomfort of being left behind, however, induces them to follow others if they think that others have tried it.

Trials by early buyers thus soften the perceived risk for followers, who are then inclined to "pile in" in their haste to buy. This forms the two tails of the distribution curve—much lower among Asian consumers—resulting in a steeper distribution curve. The left tail is longer, reflecting the hesitation to try the new product, whereas the right tail drops off sharply as consumers are ready to switch brands once the normative standards of their reference group change (see Figure 5.3).

FIGURE 5.3: *Time of adoption of innovations in an Asian context*

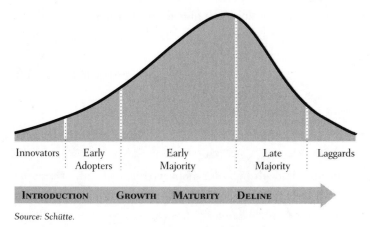

Source: Schütte.

At the time of Schütte's study no published data existed to prove the validity of a shorter and biased diffusion curve. The current study (see Figure 5.4), however, shows that for luxury products, the consumer's innovativeness is an important indicator of behavior diversity. In respect of innovativeness, the four segments are the luxury lovers, the luxury followers, the luxury intellectuals, and the luxury laggards with 15.2%, 21.9%, 35.2%, and 27.6% respectively. This finding confirmed Schütte's earlier proposition of the asymmetry of the innovations distribution curve in Asia but revealed that the curve does not end with a steeper decline, as supposed by Schütte, but with a gradual attenuation.

As noted earlier, the laggards and the intellectuals are the most loyal luxury consumers and the curve confirms this, the long and gradually declining line of the right curve representing almost 63% of luxury consumers.

FIGURE 5.4: *Time of adoption of luxury innovations in Asia*

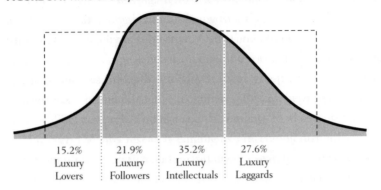

15.2%	21.9%	35.2%	27.6%
Luxury	Luxury	Luxury	Luxury
Lovers	Followers	Intellectuals	Laggards

Another interesting point concerning this curve is that the time period for a luxury innovation is longer than that of an ordinary product, such as a digital camera, which is described by the vertical broken line. It takes much longer for the luxury consumers to be informed, to discover, and to experience the innovations of luxury industry. A "star" model for a luxury brand is generally launched first in Paris or New York and introduced into the Chinese market later. Even if the launch is made almost simultaneously across the global market, the language barrier generally means that Chinese consumers receive the information later than their counterparts in Paris or New York.

Being so far removed from the new collections and from the season cycle of the fashion industry, Chinese luxury consumers are not particularly sensitive to new fashion trends. The tardiness of the Chinese luxury market toward luxury innovations ensures that the curve maintains a very long period of maturity and declines very slowly, which means that some luxury models, outdated in the West, can still be sold in Chinese boutiques.

However, as we saw earlier, Chinese consumers are very sensitive to word-of-mouth transmissions of luxury developments, even without knowing exactly what the product is. Psychologically, people are keen to pursue the new trends if only to hide their lack of knowledge of luxury products. This explains the sharp rise in the curve during the growth phase after a long period of introduction. After hearing from their friends or through the Internet that a particular product is trendy, people make the decision to buy that product. If a new brand is accepted by the luxury lovers, they become the most efficient means of communicating the brand's message in the market.

Nevertheless, for the majority of luxury lovers, luxury followers, and luxury laggards the focus is not on the concepts and the values of the new products, but merely on the fact that it is something new.

Another reason to explain the tardiness of the Chinese luxury market is the size and the nature of the market itself. There is a high degree of economic inequality between the regions. By the time the news of, say, the 2007 Paris spring-summer collections reaches the middle cities it could well be the spring of 2009. Though this will undoubtedly change with the improvement in information systems, it will take some time for Chinese luxury consumers to become attuned to the rhythms of world fashion. If you wish to become involved in the luxury industry in China, you need to be patient.

Brand loyalty and new luxury brands

Brand loyalty

Brand loyalty can be defined in terms of consumer behavior or consumer attitudes.[6] Attitudinal measures are concerned with consumers' overall feelings (i.e. evaluation) about the product and the brand, and their purchase intentions. Behavioral measures are based on observable responses to promotional stimuli—purchase behavior, rather than attitude toward the product or brand. In this study, brand loyalty measures the degree to which a consumer expresses loyalty to a luxury brand and is unwilling to even try others. Thus, it is an evaluation of the attitudes expressed by consumers, rather than of their actual purchasing behavior.

For example, the luxury laggards are the segment that has the highest brand loyalty; luxury lovers are the least loyal group and are always willing to try other brands and new products.

This is supported by the findings in this study, which showed that the degree of luxury brand loyalty in ascending order is lovers, followers, intellectuals, and laggards (see Figure 5.5).

FIGURE 5.5: *Brand loyalty indicator*

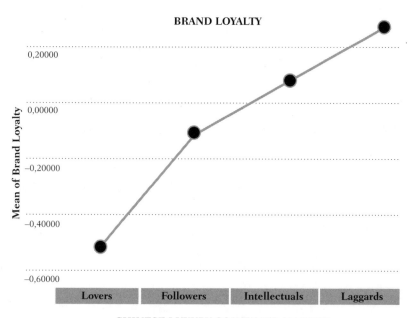

Where brand loyalty is concerned, some theorists suggest that it is correlated with the consumer's degree of involvement: high involvement leads to extensive information search and, ultimately, to brand loyalty, whereas low involvement leads to exposure and brand awareness, and then possibly to brand habit.[7] As a customer's satisfaction with a product increases along with repeated purchases, the search for information about alternative brands decreases. Previous evidence suggested that loyal consumers—those who have a strong commitment to a brand, service, or retail store—show strong resistance to counter-persuasion attempts, a conclusion confirmed in this study as well.

Innovativeness and brand loyalty

An interesting finding to emerge from our research is the negative correlation between the innovativeness of luxury products and luxury brand loyalty: the more that consumers are sensitive to the innovations of luxury products, the lower their brand loyalty will be. This result has some important implications for the luxury industry, since most luxury brands have their legendary creations with a long history behind them. The classical models of each luxury company are precious heritages and the core value of the brand: Chanel No. 5 perfume and the monogram design of Louis Vuitton's leather goods come to mind in this regard. For consumers with higher innovativeness, such as the luxury lovers, the traditional models and products of the most prestigious luxury firms may not be the most attractive products. Thus, the pursuit of innovativeness and new creations outweighs the power of brand and becomes the priority for the luxury lovers in choosing their luxury products.

However, for luxury intellectuals and laggards, classical products are more attractive than the new models, because they focus more on the functionality and quality of the brand, which has been proven over time and which they have come to trust.

Traditional luxury firms, while maintaining the loyalty of traditional luxury consumers, work on the creation of new models, the enlargement of product categories, and the utilization of new materials, which are efficient ways to attract more lovers and followers and to supply more product choices for the intellectuals and the laggards. However, for new luxury firms, innovativeness is the main and, indeed, the only point that attracts their clients, most of whom are luxury lovers or luxury followers. If the newcomers want to stay in the industry, they cannot rely solely on lovers and followers, because the consumers in these two segments are not loyal customers. It is therefore important for new luxury brands to keep their successful models and to create their own legends if they are to attract traditional luxury consumers—the intellectuals and the laggards—whose support they will need if they are to survive. Thus, a real luxury brand will have consumers from all four segments: luxury clients with very different motivations can have their various requirements met under the same brand.

Post-purchase guilt and repetitive purchase

Post-purchase guilt[8]

The notion of post-purchase guilt was developed on the basis of the cognitive dissonance theory.[9] Discomfort or dissonance occurs when a consumer holds conflicting thoughts about a belief or an object. For instance, when consumers have made a commitment—made a down-payment or placed an order for a product, particularly an expensive one such as an automobile or a luxury product—they often begin to feel a sense of unease when they think of the unique, positive qualities of the brands not selected. Though such post-purchase dissonance is quite normal, it is likely nevertheless to leave consumers with an uneasy feeling about their prior beliefs or actions—a feeling that they try to resolve by changing their attitudes in conformity with their behavior.[10]

In this study, the luxury followers are assumed to be the most dissonant segment; the luxury lovers are assumed to suffer the least (see Figure 5.6).

FIGURE 5.6: *Post-purchase guilt indicator*

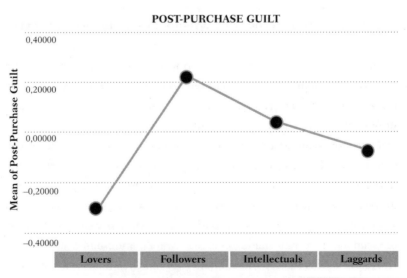

POST-PURCHASE GUILT

CHINESE LUXURY CONSUMER MARKET

What makes post-purchase dissonance relevant to marketing strategists is the premise that dissonance propels consumers to reduce the unpleasant feelings created by rival thoughts. A variety of tactics are open to consumers to reduce post-purchase dissonance. The consumer can rationalize the decision as being wise, seek out advertisements that support the choice (while avoiding dissonance-creating competitive ads), try to "sell" to friends the positive features of the brand, or look to known satisfied consumers for reassurance.[11]

In addition to such consumer-initiated tactics to reduce post-purchase uncertainty, a marketer can reduce consumer dissonance by including messages in its advertising specifically aimed at reinforcing consumers' decisions by "complimenting their wisdom,"[12] offering stronger guarantees or warranties, increasing the number and efficiency of its services, or providing detailed brochures on how to use its products correctly. Beyond these dissonance-reducing tactics, marketers are increasingly developing affinity or relationship programs designed to reward good customers and to build customer loyalty and satisfaction. As noted earlier, the luxury brand companies should also develop programs for their customers like those proposed by service-intensive industries, such as airlines, hotel chains, and major car-rental companies.[13]

For Chinese luxury consumers, post-purchase guilt is one of the most important obstacles to consuming luxury products. The psychological dissonance and inconsistency make them feel uneasy, both in making the buying decision and in the consumption of the luxury goods. As noted earlier, post-purchase guilt decreases the rate of repeat purchase and makes consumers less loyal to the brands.

For luxury followers the need to keep up with the trends and to be seen to be doing so is strong. Following the lead of the luxury lovers, they buy the most popular products of the season. However, these products soon become unfashionable, giving rise to feelings of guilt that accompanies spending a great deal of money every season. At the same time, they cannot resist the temptations of the new season, compounding their sense of guilt.

For the intellectuals, post-purchase guilt comes from conflicts between personal involvement and traditional consumption values. Since this conflict is on the psychological level, the degree of guilt they experience is much lower than that of the followers.

The task of the luxury firms is to decrease the level of post-purchase guilt experienced by these two segments. Since the reasons for their dissonance are different, the methods to combat them should also be different. For the followers, the best way to do this is to change their choices of products: offering them more classical models will prolong the product life and enable trendy people to feel neither unfashionable nor too fashionable. This could also result in increasing their loyalty to the luxury brand. Once they feel comfortable in choosing the classical model, they may gradually change their buying behavior and progress to the intellectual category: a loyal consumer of the luxury brand.

For intellectuals, adding more services during the act of purchasing may decrease customers' dissonance when they buy a luxury product. The added services may differ according to the customs of each luxury firm: offering a free drink while the customer is waiting, the personalization of the purchased item, a customer loyalty scheme, and so on.

Geographic locations: Beijing/Shanghai/ Guangzhou/Chengdu

It is wrong to think of China as being a homogeneous market, especially in the luxury industry. There are so many geographical, cultural, and linguistic differences within the one country that it would be a mistake to impose one single approach to marketing.

There is a plethora of languages and dialects and though the Mainland has, since 1953, shared a simplified written form of language the traditional writing system is still used in Hong Kong and Taiwan. That is why luxury houses have to develop two Web sites with these two writing systems for their Chinese clients.

To get a better understanding of the differences in consumer behavior that arise from China's geographical diversity, we split the Mainland market into four regions with shared characteristics: North, East, South,

TABLE 5.1: *Principal distribution networks, by region*

Region Metropolis	Provinces, Municipalities, and Autonomic zones	Secondary Cities	Tier Cities
North **Beijing**	Beijing		
	Tianjin	Tianjin	
	Liaoning	Dalian, Shenyang	
	Heilongjiang	Haerbin	
	Jilin	Changchun	
	Shanxi	Taiyuan	
	Hebei		Shijiazhuang, Tangshan
	Henan		Zhengzhou
	Inner Mongolia		
East **Shanghai, Hangzhou**	Shanghai		
	Zhejiang	Wenzhou, Ningbo	Jiaxing, Huzhou, Shaoxing, Yiwu, Taizhou
	Jiangsu	Suzhou, Wuxi, Nanjing	Changzhou, Xuzhou
	Fujian	Fuzhou, Xiamen	
	Shandong	Qingdao, Jinan	Yantai, Zibo
	Anhui		Hefei
	Jiangxi		Nanchang
South **Guangzhou**	Guangdong	Shenzhen, Zhuhai, Shantou	Zhongshan, Foshan, Dongguan
	Hubei	Wuhan	
	Nunnan	Kunming	
	Hunan	Changsha	
	Hannan	Haikou, Sanya	
	Guangxi		Nanning, Guilin
	Hong Kong*		
	Macao*		
	Taiwan**		
Middle and West **Chengdou**	Sichuan		
	Chongqing	Chongqing	
	Shannxi	Xian	
	Guizhou		Guiyang
	Ganzu		Lanzhou
	Ningxia		Yinchuan
	Qinghai		Xining
	Xinjiang		Urumqi
	Tibet		Lasa

* *Special Administration Zones*   ** *Taiwan is part of, but not administered by, the Mainland*

and Middle & West. Within each, one central city has been selected to represent the region as a whole.

In each region, there are a number of secondary cities which also play an important role in luxury retailing and distribution. Note that in the Eastern region Zhejiang province, south of Shanghai, is also economically very well developed and people love luxury brands; thus, its capital, Hangzhou, is ranked alongside Shanghai because many luxury companies consider Hangzhou as a priority when it comes to setting up their boutiques. For example, the biggest Louis Vuitton store in China is located there.

Table 5.1 provides an overview of the principal cities of value to luxury companies in developing their distribution networks.

Table 5.2 shows the regional distribution of the four luxury segments.

TABLE 5.2: *Luxury segments: distribution by region*

Region	Luxury Lovers	Luxury Followers	Luxury Intellectuals	Luxury Laggards	Total
Beijing (North)	15.6%	15.6%	42.2%	26.5%	100%
Shanghai (East)	13%	26.1%	33.7%	27.2%	100%
Guangzhou (South)	22.5%	27.5%	30%	20%	100%
Chengdu (Middle & West)	3.3%	33.3%	16.7%	46.7%	100%

A breakdown by major metropolis is given in Figure 5.7. The differences between the groups are significant: Guangzhou has approximately 50% luxury lovers and luxury followers compared to Beijing's 31%. Beijing has the greatest concentration of intellectuals (42%), while Chengdu has the greatest concentration of laggards (46%).

This indicates that the South and East of China have more luxury consumers whose behavior is focused on social influences: that is, they are generally more conspicuous in their consumption than the people from the North and the Middle. In seeking an explanation for these differences, in the next section we will examine the cultural and historical backgrounds, the economic development, and the local lifestyles and mentalities of each of these major regional cities.

FIGURE 5.7: *Luxury segment breakdown, by major metropolis*

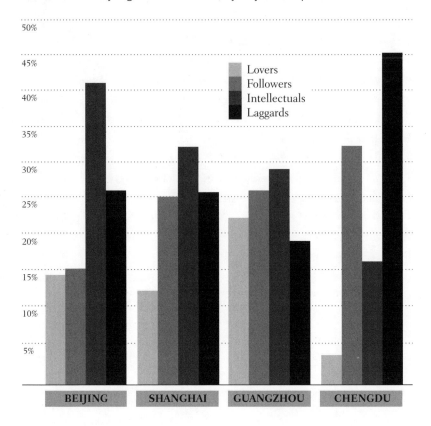

Beijing and the North

Geography and demographics

Beijing sits in the northeastern corner of China and has been the nation's capital for most of the past 700 years, since Kublai Khan first established his court there. The center of town is the Forbidden City, home of the emperors and off-limits to ordinary Chinese until the Communist Revolution in 1949. All the central government organizations, ministries, military, and media groups are concentrated around the Forbidden City. Because of downtown space limitations, the CBD developed in the eastern suburbs of Beijing and it has become the most vivid and modern side of the city and home to most of the landmark luxury businesses.

Beijing is the second-largest city in China, lagging behind only Shanghai in economic and industrial production. However, its service and finance sectors between them contribute 76% of Beijing's GDP. The financial sector controls more than 90% of the nation's credit capital and 65% of its insurance capital. Of the 500 biggest multinational companies, 293 have their Greater China or Asia-Pacific headquarters in Beijing, according to *Fortune* magazine.

Beijing is unrivaled in the number of colleges and universities it has, including China's two most prestigious institutions, Peking University, and Tsinghua University. More than 15% of Chinese universities and 60% of national research centers are located here and many multinational companies also have research centers here. The city is also the art, media, and sports center of China, creating a very rich and vivid cultural environment.

In 2005, the nation's capital had a total population of 15.38 million, of which 11.87 million had permanent residence (*hukou*).

The city's luxury consumers include high-level government officials, CEOs of state-owned banks and companies, successful businessmen, movie and sports stars, high-tech yuppies, and tourists. Luxury consumers also incorporate institutions, such as lobbyists and governmental organizations.

Macroeconomic review

In 2005, Beijing's nominal GDP was RMB681.45 billion (about US$84 billion), a year-on-year growth of 11.1% from the previous year. Its GDP per capita was RMB44,969, an increase of 8.1% from the previous year and nearly twice as much as in 2000. Beijing's primary, secondary, and tertiary industries were worth RMB9.77 billion, RMB210.05 billion, and RMB461.63 billion, respectively. Urban disposable income per capita was RMB17,653, a real increase of 12.9% over the previous year. The per-capita income of rural residents was RMB7,860, a real increase of 9.6%. The disposable income of the 20% low-income residents increased by 16.7%, 11.4 percentage points higher than the growth rate of the 20% high-income residents.

Beijing's real estate and automobile sectors have continued to blossom in recent years. In 2005, a total of 28,032 million square meters of housing real estate was sold, at a total value of RMB175.88 billion. The number of automobiles registered in 2004 was 2,146,000, of which 1,540,000 were privately-owned (a year-on-year increase of 18.7%).

TABLE 5.3: *Beijing's economic performance 2001–2005*

	2001	2002	2003	2004	2005
GDP Growth	11.0%	10.2%	10.5%	13.2%	11.1%
China GDP	7.3%	8.9%	9.1%	9.5%	9.9%
Retail Sales Growth	10.4%	9.5%	14.5%	15.3%	10.8%

Source: Beijing Bureau of Statistics.

The main commercial areas

As a political and cultural center, commerce seems to take second place in the municipality's priority list. However, the consumer market is huge and the five main commercial areas are very active.

The Beijing CBD, centered at the Guomao area and linked with the silk market and Soho city areas, is home to a variety of corporate regional headquarters, shopping malls, and high-end housing. The headquarters of Motorola and HP, the new Chinese Central Television Center (CCTV), the new Beijing television center (BTV), and the Beijing media group's headquarters are also in the heart of the area.

The Lufthansa area is a high-end shopping district surrounded by the diplomatic district, corporate centers, and luxury hotels. The Wangfujing and Xidan areas are major traditional shopping districts, and Financial Street is the traditional financial center.

Zhongguancun, dubbed "China's Silicon Valley," continues to be a major center for electronics- and computer-related industries, as well as pharmaceuticals-related research. Numbers of colleges, universities, and research institutes are located in the area, as well as major enterprises such as Microsoft, Google, and many NASDAQ-listed Chinese dot-com companies.

The luxury shopping blocks

The major centers for luxury shopping are concentrated in the CBD (the China World Trade Center) and Wangfujing (the Peninsula Palace Hotel). Some new landmarks are under construction in preparation for the Olympic Games in 2008. These include Shin Kong Place in the CBD and Seasons Place in Financial Street.

The Peninsula Palace Hotel (Wang Fu Hotel) is one of the first five-star luxury hotels in Mainland China. Its strategic location near the Forbidden City and Tiananmen Square meant that it quickly became a landmark for many luxury companies seeking to develop a market in China. In the late '80s and early '90s it was the only place to be profitable for a luxury brand in China and companies such as Hermès, Louis Vuitton, Chanel, Zegna, and Prada had their first experience of the Chinese luxury market from the shopping mall of the Peninsula Palace.

Despite the fact that the biggest store in the mall cannot exceed 300 square meters, it is the dream of every luxury brand to have a pied à terre there.

Like the Peninsula, Oriental Plaza (Dong Fang Square) is located in the Wangfujing area, on the north side of Chang'an Avenue, the longest street in the world. Built by Hong Kong tycoon Lee Ka Shing, this project has established itself as the most visited shopping mall in Beijing, with millions of domestic and international tourists every year. The ground floor of the plaza is occupied by the likes of Zegna, Valentino, Burberry, MaxMara, Bally, Dunhill, Tiffany, Kenzo, Jaeger-LeCoultre, S.T. Dupont, and Rolex, to name but a few.

The China World Trade Center has been another landmark for luxury business in Beijing since the early 1990s. High-end offices, a five-star hotel, luxury serviced apartments, and a luxury shopping mall have grown up around it and it has become a center of selective retailing, with many of the top brand names establishing stores there, including Louis Vuitton, Hermès, Gucci, Dior, Dunhill, Prada, Salvatore Ferragamo, Cartier, Van Cleef & Arpels, and many more.

The Scitech Center (Sai Te), located on the west side of the CBD in the old embassy district, and Shin Kong Place, on the east side, have become the haunts of the young and fashionable, from local businessmen to movie stars, and this is reflected in the large number of luxury brands to be found there.

The Lufthansa Center (Yan Sha), located on the north side of the CBD, houses a number of embassies, high-end office buildings, five-star hotels, luxury serviced apartments, and international schools.

Seasons Place is the only shopping mall in Neijing's Financial Street. All of the major Chinese banks and insurance companies have their head-quarters here and the Ritz-Carlton, Westin, and Intercontinental hotels all chose this area to open their first five-star hotels in Beijing.

Seasons Place mall was well positioned to take advantage of the boom in the Chinese stock market that began in October 1996 and has since created fortunes for tens of thousands of traders who immediately became the best clients of the luxury industry. Louis Vuitton is opening its third Beijing store in the mall.

Consumer culture and luxury lifestyle

Beijing is a city with a very strong culture of fine arts. Descendants of royal families and ministers, artists, and scholars have created the art of life of Beijing. They were very good at 吃、喝、玩、乐，*chi, he, wan, le*—wining and dining, leisure and happiness, beer and skittles—and many traditional Chinese luxury brands were created with the craftsmanship of artisans in every aspect of daily life: Tongshenghe for clothing; Buyingzhai for shoes; Quanjude, Donglaishun, and Fangshan for high-class restaurants; Rong-baozhai for writing instruments; Tongrentang for Chinese medicines … the list goes on. The people of Beijing are very familiar with luxurious living and have a great love of finely crafted objects, as witnessed at the Rongbaozhai fine art studios in Liulichang and the Paijiayuan market, which attracts domestic and overseas fine-art collectors.

Consumption characteristics and consumer personalities

The luxury culture of Beijing reflects wealth, power, and social influence. The city has significantly more luxury intellectuals than any other city: while they enjoy luxury products and brands, they also appreciate the his-tory, values, and culture which underpin those brands.

Initially, they maintain a distance from the international luxury brands as they witness the brands' evolution. If the brand fits them well after this trial period, they take it up very quickly. There is also an element of self-importance in the behavior of the intellectuals in disdaining things with which they are not familiar. They don't make imprudent decisions and want to be sure about the result.

Because the potential market population can be measured in millions, brands have to be sure that their image and product information are communicated correctly within the market to reach the right person in the right place at the right time.

But new luxury brands have to be patient, as Helene Zhang, marketing manager of Givenchy China and former PR manager of Guerlain China, noted: "Beijing consumers are quite conservative when they meet an unknown luxury brand. It takes time and a strong marketing campaign to communicate your brand and reach your targeted clients effectively. Once they are very well informed and accept your brand, they move very fast and their buying power is the highest in China."[14]

Brands such as Louis Vuitton and Hermès are now so well known that when new collections come out their clients move very fast, says Ming Zhao, national retailing manager of Hermès China: "Our Beijing clients are very sensitive to products with artistic elements and designs ... because there are lots of clients with strong cultural and artistic backgrounds who understand well the concept of our designers and the spirit of fine art of our brand."[15]

While wealth is one way to prove social success, it is not the only way, because Beijing is, first and foremost, the political center of China. Before wealth, power is the priority. An excessive display of personal wealth can, in fact, bring problems if it creates jealousy from politicians and the military. Successful businessmen, movie stars, and sports personalities are well-advised to be discreet and to become involved in government-organized social activities. In fact, it is not unusual in this city to meet millionaires dressed in a T-shirt, old jeans, and dirty sport shoes queuing alongside everyone else at the local Starbuck's.

Beijing's consumers are less sensitive toward the price of a luxury product than consumers in other cities, such as Shanghai or Canton. The fact that a particular luxury item can be purchased for less elsewhere is of less importance than the pride that comes with owning it before most others. The northern Chinese do not like to be seen as penny-pinchers. They are often generous and broad-minded. As Helene Zhang puts it: "Our clients in Beijing are cool. They support us every time in our marketing activities and have lots of fun. Everybody wants to buy our new product, because we have a very strong and positive brand image for them."[16]

Shanghai and the East

Geography and demographics

Shanghai means "City on the Sea," and the sea has indeed brought Shanghai much of its considerable wealth over the ages; from the old silk and opium trade to its present role as the country's leading manufacturing center and a port that handles almost a third of China's trade. Shanghai is located on the Yangtze Delta which incorporates the industrial, agricultural, and commercial bases of Zhejiang, Jiangsu, Anhui, and Jiangxi provinces.

Shanghai's history can be seen along the Bund, the waterfront boulevard that hosts magnificent hotels and banks overlooking the new commercial area of Pudong. From humble beginnings as a fishing village, Shanghai has become one of the world's busiest ports (in 2005, it handled a total of 443 million tons of cargo). As a tourist city, each year it brings millions of travelers from both home and abroad, attracted by its commercial activity and opportunities rather than its scenic beauty.

Macroeconomic review

Being the only large central Chinese port not cut off from the interior by mountains, Shanghai is the natural gateway to the Chang basin, one of China's richest regions. It handles much of the country's foreign shipping and a large coastal trade. Great sums are expended to keep open its continually silting harbor. Although water transport is of prime importance, highways radiate outward, and there are rail connections with Nanjing and

Hangzhou and, through them, to the North and South China networks. A new international airport opened in Pudong (East Shanghai) in 1999.

Despite lacking its own supplies of fuel and raw materials, Shanghai is China's leading industrial city, with large steelworks, textile mills, ship-building yards, and oil-refining and gas-extracting operations. Its other activities include a range of heavy and light industry, electronics and computer equipment, chemicals, pharmaceuticals, aircraft, motor vehicles, plastics, and consumer goods. The city is also a major publishing center. Shanghai includes much of the surrounding rural area, where farms produce the food that supports the city's population.

In the 1970s and '80s, Shanghai's industrial base was shifted to include more light industries in order to reduce pollution. There was much rebuilding and expansion; new factories emerged around the outskirts of the city, and the northwest section was developed as an industrial district. Development in the 1990s concentrated on the special economic development zone of Pudong, an area formerly dominated by farms and marshland. The 1990s also brought new bridges and tunnels and a subway system.

Though the official registered population as of 2005 was 17.42 million, there are more than five million other people living, unregistered, in the city, the vast majority of whom form a floating population of temporary migrant workers from Anhui, Jiangsu, and Zhejiang provinces.

Shanghai rivals Hong Kong as the economic center of China. The city had a per-capita GDP equivalent to US$7,116 in 2006, the highest of all Chinese cities. Shanghai has increased its role in finance and banking, and as a major destination for corporate headquarters, fueling demand for a highly educated and modernized workforce. Shanghai recorded double-digit growth for 14 consecutive years since major reforms began in the city in 1992. In 2005, its nominal GDP posted an 11.3% growth to RMB915.4 billion (US$117 billion).

According to the latest data from the Shanghai Statistics Bureau, the city's economic growth continued its rapid pace and, in 2007, recorded a GDP growth figure of 13.3%. Foreign investment remains the major driver of the economy. With increased government control, economic growth is focusing on quality rather than speed.

TABLE 5.4: *Shanghai's economic indicators*

	2001	2002	2003	2004	2005
GDP Growth	10.20%	10.90%	11.80%	13.60%	11.10% (RMB 914.39 billion)
Permanent Population Growth	N.A.	N.A.	5.29%	2.40%	2.07% (17.42 million)
Retail Sales Growth	8.1%	9.3%	9.1%	10.5%	11.5%
CPI Growth	0.70%	-0.80%	1.20%	2.20%	1.00%
Av. Disposal Income Growth	9.94%	2.85%	12.20%	12.21%	10.9% (RMB10,704)

Source: Shanghai Statistics Bureau.

The commercial areas

The city's commercial section, the former International Settlement, is modern and Western in appearance, with broad streets and boulevards (including The Bund, Nanjing Road, and Bubbling Well Road) lined with imposing buildings. Typical Asian buildings are found only in the original Chinese town, known as Nanshi.

Next to Beijing, Shanghai is the country's foremost educational center and houses Fudan University, Jiaotong University, Tongji University, three medical colleges, and numerous technological and scientific institutes. Shanghai has an astronomical observatory and many research institutes and learned societies. People's Square, refurbished in the late 1990s, is the site of an opera house designed by Charpentier, a renown French architect, and a museum containing the country's finest collection of Chinese art.

Shanghai is administratively equal to a province and is divided into 19 county-level divisions. There is no single downtown district in Shanghai, the urban core being scattered across several districts. Nine of the districts on the west bank are collectively referred to as the core city of Shanghai. Prominent central business areas include Lujiazui on the east bank of the Huangpu River, and The Bund and Hongqiao areas on the west bank. The city hall and major administration units are located in Huangpu District, which also serves as a commercial area, including the famous Nanjing Road. Other major commercial areas include the classy Xintiandi and Huaihai Road in Luwan district and Xujiahui in Xuhui District.

China's premier shopping street, East Nanjing Road, begins from the Yuyuan Bazaar (famous for Chinese crafts and jewelry) and its long pedestrian boulevard lined with busy shops is often packed with people on weekends and holidays. The shops are often targeted at domestic tourists, so the prices are surprisingly reasonable.

Shanghainese locals shop at Huaihai Road, which is celebrated for its elegance and features most of the local top-end designer brands. North Sichuan Road also offers good, inexpensive merchandise and is always popular among young people.

The luxury shopping blocks

For the luxury brands, generally speaking, there are five main areas: The Bund, West Nanjing Road, Xintiandi, Hongqiao, and Pudong. Here, all of the major international brands found in Beijing can be found. Giorgio Armani, Hugo Boss, and Dolce & Gabanna all have flagship stores on The Bund, which is also home to some of the trendiest bars and restaurants.

However, the problem with The Bund is that it is noisy, always crowded with Chinese tourists, the majority of whom are there for the views of the Huangpu River, not for shopping.

Middle Huaihai Road and Xintiandi offer high-end shopping typified by the international-style department stores in the former French Concession area. Shanghai Tang, Aston Martin, and Tourneau, the American timepiece retailer, all chose the Xintiandi area for their flagship stores.

Consumer culture and luxury lifestyle

One of Shanghai's most famous cultural artifacts is the cheongsam. Though the Cultural Revolution brought a temporary end to this and other Shanghai fashions, they have enjoyed a revival since 1979. In the past decade, in fact, the fashion industry has revitalized to the point where today there is, on average, one fashion show per day in Shanghai. Reflecting Shanghai's architecture, local fashion designers strive to create a fusion of Western and traditional designs, often with innovative if not controversial results. Shanghai Tang's collections and colors are mostly inspired by the styles of 1930s Shanghai.

Shanghai is a comparatively young city which began to grow with the concessions given to Westerners following the First Opium War in 1840. The many late-19th- and early-20th-century Western-style buildings in downtown Shanghai are a legacy of this period. This cultural background has influenced very deeply the way Shanghai's consumers think and behave.

The Chinese idiom "worship and have blind faith in foreign things" is one very much taken to heart by the people of Shanghai, who are very positive toward imported products of any kind. They look down on Chinese-made products; for them, "foreign goods" connotes good quality and fashion. The Shanghainese, who are quick to take up luxury brands, are more luxury lovers and followers than intellectuals. They are great readers of fashion magazines and believe what they are told there, making them very sensitive to the latest trends.

Contrary to the general image of Shanghai as a city of potential and opportunities, native Shanghainese are not great risk-takers. In fact, the opportunities offered by the city have, for the most part, been created by people from outside—through foreign investment and central government policies—and taken up by people from outside—by businessmen from overseas and from Hong Kong and Taiwan. The upper-middle class and super-rich in Shanghai are, in fact, mostly from Zhejiang and Jiangsu provinces and the huge expatriate community also provides great purchasing power. The local Shanghainese prefer stability in employment to more risk-driven positions.

Buying foreign brands is, in a way, another manifestation of this preference for stability and a way of avoiding risk. The Shanghainese trust the concept of brand as a guarantee of quality and as a means of gaining face in front of friends.

Consumption characteristics and consumer personalities

As mentioned earlier, in Chinese terms, Shanghai is a young city with a short history. Its culture is a mixture of semi-feudal and colonial elements, which makes it quite different from most other major cities. This limited history may explain why Shanghai is so forward-looking in its attitudes, particularly in its approach to luxury. Michelle Chen, marketing and retailing director of Ports 1961, describes the differences between Shanghai's luxury consumers and those of Beijing this way: "In general, Shanghai consumers know very well what they are buying as a luxury brand or product … Beijing consumers rely more on personal experience and the feelings towards the products and brands, instead of following others."[17]

The show-off in Shanghai is much more extravagant than in Beijing, because he is further away from politics and the central government. The core interest of local people is money and there is no need to be discreet. There are so many young girls with Louis Vuitton and Gucci bags in the lobby of Plaza 66 that it seems the bags are obligatory for anyone wishing to shop there.

The imitation effect works very well in Shanghai. If a particular product becomes trendy and popular, everybody wants to have one. In such circumstances, if you want to show how special you are, there are always the "limited collections" and "special collections" to acquire. As Hermès retailing manager Ming Zhao puts it: "Shanghainese prefer flashy and trendy models, but in Beijing they love models with more cultural content and classical designs."[18]

Price is always a sensitive issue for the Shanghainese, even for luxury goods. They are always looking for the best value for money, which is not a common feature of the luxury industry since the value of a luxury product consists not only of the materials, but also of the design and the emotion involved in their possession. Given this, you may wonder why so many luxury brands have their flagship stores in Shanghai. The answer is simple: to do luxury business in China, you should appear to be very successful in Shanghai, even if your beautiful flagship store on The Bund is losing money, in order to develop your retailing network in the other cities. If you look at the clients of luxury boutiques in Shanghai, lots of consumers are from Zhejiang and Jiangsu provinces, China's two richest provinces. All the super-rich families from these provinces own companies and houses in Shanghai.

The number of real Shanghainese luxury consumers is comparatively limited, and generally comprise professionals working for international companies and state-owned companies, or owners of a private business or speculators on the financial market. But together with the rich provincial families and vast numbers of expatriates, they make up a huge luxury market.

Many fashionable young Shanghainese women working as clerks and secretaries are by no means affluent but, being exposed on a daily basis to a luxury environment, feel it necessary for their self-confidence to own at least a luxury handbag. Often, they obtain such items in Hong Kong, where the prices for luxury goods and cosmetics can be as much as 50% cheaper, more than covering the cost of travel.

Guangzhou and the South

Geography

Formerly known in the West as "Canton," Guangzhou is the capital of Guangdong Province, in southern China. Located on the Pearl River delta about 120 km northwest of Hong Kong, it is an important trading center. With a population of 9.7 million at the end 2006, it is the third-most populous metropolitan area in Mainland China.

Like Athens and Rome, Guangzhou has a history spanning thousands of years and legends and monuments from its democratic and revolutionary past are plentiful. The anti-British struggle at San Yuan Li in 1841 is marked by a monument and the Huang Hua Gang Park keeps alive the spirit of the 72 martyrs killed in a 1911 uprising against the Manchu dynasty.

Guangzhou is also one of the most important centers of foreign commerce in South China, hosting the Chinese Export Commodities Fair twice a year since 1957. It is also a cultural center and home to several universities.

Guangzhou ranks first in the number of restaurants and tea-houses in the country and Cantonese cuisine is famous for its color, fragrance, taste, and presentation. Guangzhou is the communication hub of Guangdong

Province, with railways and highways radiating in all directions, and convenient inland-water, coastal, and ocean transport. Efforts are being made to build Guangzhou into an international metropolis functioning primarily as the biggest financial, high-tech, and light industrial center in South China.

Macroeconomic review

Guangzhou is a special economic development zone and an important trading point. In 2003, the GDP in the province hit US$191.4 billion, considerably higher than that of Hong Kong (US$158 billion) and was expected to surpass that of Taiwan (US$376.6 billion) in 2007. Statistics show that in 2005, the per-capita GDP in Guangdong was US$2,980.

The three pillar industries are the information technology, automobile, and petrochemical industries, accounting for 30% of the city's gross industrial output in 2006 and generating a total value of RMB84.8 billion. The year also witnessed rapid growth in post and telecommunications, merchandise circulation, communication and transportation, tourism, real estate, and social services. As much as 55.9% of the economic growth has resulted from the development of tertiary industry. Total revenue was RMB75.63 billion, up 25.8% on the previous year.

The total retail value of consumer goods reached RMB124.39 billion in 2005, up 11% on the previous year. The per-capita disposable income of residents in the city proper came to RMB14,416, up 5.8%, and there was a 1.4% increase in per-capita spending on consumer goods such as housing, private cars, and education.

The Chinese Export Commodities Fair—the Canton Fair—is held each spring and autumn. Inaugurated in the spring of 1957, the Fair attracts businessmen from all over the world. Even during the Cultural Revolution, the Canton Fair remained active and for almost 20 years was the only door opened to the world market, primarily through Hong Kong.

Main commercial areas

There are three main commercial areas in Guangzhou: Beijing Street, Shangxiajiu pedestrian precinct, and the Tianhe City area.

Beijing Street is the main shopping thoroughfare, where most stores are open from 9am to 10pm. Mayflower Plaza at the northern end of the street is a place where young people hang out and shop. Shangxiajiu Street is a very popular shopping area and a showcase for traditional Cantonese architecture. Prices here are generally lower than in Beijing Street, where Liwan Plaza is the main shopping center.

The newly developed shopping area of Tianhe City has the Grandbuy Zhengjia Plaza, the largest Western-style shopping mall in China, Tee Mall, which is probably the busiest and most popular shopping mall in the heart of the city, and the Zhong Tian Shopping Plaza located at Citic.

Luxury shopping

The best locations for luxury brands are in the Huanshi East Road area, where the Garden Hotel, Baiyun Hotel, World Trade Shopping Mall, and Friendship Store are located. The luxury landmark here is La Perle, which houses all of the big-name brands. The Friendship Store is a traditional shopping center targeting foreigners and affluent Cantonese. Here, too, the usual top-name brands can be found.

Consumer culture and luxury lifestyle

Guangzhou has a long history of engaging in commerce and is regarded as the earliest among the world's international trading ports. Built as Chuting by the Chu people on the middle reaches of the Yangtze River in the ninth century BC, it became the starting point of the Silk Road and China's only foreign trade port before the Qing dynasty. Because of this long history of international commerce and its proximity, geographically and culturally, to Hong Kong and Macao, it is familiar with influences from the Western world.

As a major entry point for overseas culture for many centuries, foreigners are not the anomaly here that they are in other Chinese cities. Consequently, travelers are afforded more personal space and freedom. Guangzhou also boasts the largest urban park in China, an island of refurbished colonial buildings and some world-class galleries and exhibition spaces. In addition, possibly due to the distance from the country's political centers, the citizens of Guangzhou have developed a laid-back and play-hard approach to life.

The Cantonese accept both luxury brands and the Western luxury lifestyle, incorporating sports such as golf and tennis. Indeed, it is now a venue for the Tennis Masters Cup, one of the top tennis tournaments in the world.

However, as far as the luxury industry is concerned, Guangzhou suffers from its proximity to Hong Kong, where luxury products are at least 20% cheaper. The fact that most of the city's luxury consumers prefer to do their shopping in Hong Kong explains why there are fewer international luxury brands to be found in Guangzhou than in Beijing or Shanghai.

Consumption characteristics and consumer personalities

As a result of its history and geographical positioning, Guangzhou looks much more to Hong Kong, Macao, Taiwan, and Southeast Asia than to Northern China for its cultural influences. The Cantonese receive early exposure to luxury products primarily through Hong Kong.

As the focus of economic opening after 1979, this part of South China benefited early from foreign investment and international commerce. Not surprisingly, the first of China's affluent and super-rich emerged in Guangzhou and in the Guangdong area. The Cantonese tend to be proud of their culture and their achievements and this is reflected in their attitudes and behavior, which are seen in northern China as being arrogant and self-oriented. Mention the "new rich" in China in general and a picture emerges of the Cantonese businessman with his big gold necklace, gold ring, and gold Rolex—the epitome of conspicuous consumption.

The Shanghainese often see themselves as the trendiest people in China, but when it comes to the speed at which new products are adopted the Cantonese are streets ahead. They are the true risk-takers, prepared to try anything new—from famous and new brands alike. This is reflected in the fact that Dior started to sell cosmetics from Guangzhou as early as 1985, and Rémy Martin sold its first bottle of Cognac in the White Swan Hotel Guangzhou, China's first five-star hotel, in 1983. Of China's four

special economic zones, three (Shenzhen, Zhuhai, Shantou) are located
in Guangdong Province, which has had a profound influence on lifestyles
and luxury consumption there.

Chengdu and the Middle West

Geography

Chengdu, in China's southwest, is the capital of Sichuan Province and,
with 9.2 million people, is the fifth-most populous city in the country.
Its agricultural wealth has earned Chengdu the title of "Land of Milk
and Honey."

Macroeconomic review

Chengdu is the economic hub of Middle and Western China with a
GDP of RMB275 billion (about US$36 billion) and a per-capita GDP of
RMB25,950 (US$3,500).

Sichuan Province and the Chengdu region have long been the capital of traditional Chinese medicine and the city has become one of the
major pharmaceutical R&D centers in China. It is also renowned as a
national base for the electronics and IT industries, attracting a variety of
multinationals such as Intel, IBM, NOKIA, Alcatel, Motorola, SAP, and
Microsoft, as well as domestic powerhouses such as Lenovo.

Chengdu—the home of the first paper currency in 1023, during the
Song dynasty—is also becoming the financial hub in Western China for
domestic financial firms and a host of major international financial institutions that include Citigroup, HSBC, Standard Chartered Bank, United
Overseas Bank (Singapore), ABN AMRO, and Bank of East Asia.

Main commercial areas

Going to Chengdu without visiting Chunxi Road is like going to Paris
without visiting the Champs-Elysées or New York without seeing 5th
Avenue. With a 70-year history, Chunxi Road boasts department stores,
boutiques, and modern cafes.

The Yanshikou commercial circle, with the People's Department Store, Chengdu Department Emporium, and Renhe Spring Department Store, also has a great deal to offer in the way of shopping.

Luxury shopping

In Chengdu, the three luxury shopping blocks—Renhe Spring Department Store, Maison Mode, and Seibu Department Store— offer a range of international brands, including Prada, Burberry, Cartier, Dior, Dunhill, Hermès, Gucci, Salvatore Ferragamo, Versace, Ermenegildo Zegna, and many more.

Consumer culture and luxury lifestyle

Chengdu was recently named China's fourth-most livable city by *China Daily*. The city's location and an abundance of natural resources give Chengdu people a relaxed, leisure-oriented lifestyle. The people don't appear to suffer the stresses of business and international competition and maintain the gentler rhythms of a lifestyle which incorporates visits to tea houses and games of mahjong as part of the daily flow. It is not only in this relaxed approach to things that the people of Chengdu are similar to Parisians. They too take their food seriously and, like Parisians, are in the front line of fashion.

Consumption characteristics and consumer personalities

The luxury consumers in Chengdu are very young, even younger than the national average for luxury consumers. Young people in the city are very sensitive to fashion and luxury goods, Western lifestyles, popular cultural events, and entertainments. Their purchasing power is very strong and will become stronger as they get older and their incomes increase. For these consumers, price is not really an issue when they love an object.

However, older affluent consumers in Chengdu prefer a more leisurely life of tea and mahjong rather than spending money on luxury goods. Most of the millionaires dress very simply and often in Chinese style, unlike their flashier counterparts in Shanghai and Guangzhou. They are more concerned with good quality and lower price, focusing on function rather than brand; which explains why there are more luxury laggards here. Their existence is expressed through internal elements more than material appearance. However, they are prepared to spend millions on culture-related products, such as a painting or object d'art, or a villa near a historical site, for example.

Counterfeit luxury products[19]

In this section, we focus on a very important issue in the luxury industry: counterfeiting. However, rather than simply blaming the counterfeiters, we examine the other side of the supply-demand chain—the consumers— and try to understand their motivations and the implications for the luxury brands.

The problem of counterfeit luxury goods is by no means new and shows no sign of slowing down in the foreseeable future. More than a decade ago, the global trade in counterfeit goods of all kinds was estimated to be around US$299 billion, representing about 5–7% of world trade.[20] More recent estimates put the cost of luxury counterfeiting alone at around US$4.3 billion in lost sales each year.[21] The counterfeiters' activities not only damage intellectual property rights (trademarks, patents, and copyrights) but also cause important job losses (200,000 job losses in the U.S. and Europe in 1998 and 750,000 job losses in the world).[22]

In this regard, there have been trends which were anticipated by neither the luxury industry nor by market researchers. Some 20 years ago, counterfeit goods were reserved for consumers who couldn't afford the genuine article and often those buyers had to go to specific locations (for example, certain Asian or North African countries) to find the goods. Today, these goods are sold everywhere, from New York to Milan or from Tokyo to Paris, not to mention Bangkok and Shanghai. Most luxury brands are subject to counterfeiting, the extent of which depends on the popularity and desirability of their products and on prevailing attitudes toward lawfulness.[23]

One study found that about two-thirds of respondents indicated that the value, satisfaction, and status of the original luxury goods were not decreased by the availability of counterfeits; a little more than half did not believe that counterfeits affected demand for the original.[24] Generally, consumers believe counterfeits are of lower quality and higher in defects.[25] However, one important issue that such studies did not take into consideration was that today's luxury counterfeited goods are, in fact, of a much higher quality. Indeed, the level of counterfeit has become so sophisticated that only an expert eye can tell the fake from the real. With this increased sophistication in the manufacture of luxury counterfeits, the consumer's motivation to buy those goods will also become more complex than previous studies seem to indicate.

Previous research into luxury counterfeiting has focused directly on the effects this has had on the value of the luxury brands or on how to reduce demand for counterfeit products. Very little attention has been paid to the motivations of the buyers in buying the counterfeits.

To fill the void, we undertook a qualitative study using focus groups of buyers and non-buyers of counterfeited luxury goods. The focus groups, in Beijing and Shanghai, consisted of 30 people (18 women and 12 men) aged from 20 to 47 years. All were professionals with different income levels. Similar research was conducted in Japan and Europe by my research colleague Dr. Michel Phan, assistant professor of Essec Paris-Singapore.

Consumers may purchase counterfeits knowing them to be such or they may be deceived into buying them believing them to be genuine. For the purposes of our study, we treated both the same because in most cases the products (counterfeit or not) were bought in places outside of the selective retailing system that luxury brands usually inhabit. Normally, a luxury consumer will be well aware of the official luxury stores.

In consumer behavior research, motivation is described as a driving force within individuals that impels them to action. This driving force is produced by a state of tension, which exists as the result of an unfulfilled need. Individuals strive both consciously and subconsciously to reduce this tension through behavior that they anticipate will fulfill their needs and thus relieve them of the stress they feel. The unfulfilled needs, wants, and desires are translated as motivations which drive the consumer's behavior.

Unfulfilled needs, wants, and desires

The unfulfilled needs of a buyer of counterfeits are not innate: the counterfeits cannot fulfill any primary needs or motives for the consumers.

For them the needs are generally psychological—to do with self-esteem, prestige, affection, power, and learning—acquired in response to the culture or environment. The acquired needs result from the individual's subjective psychological state and from relationships with others, such as social needs, ego needs, or secondary needs.[26]

Motivations

Motives are difficult to identify and measure, and it is also difficult to know which motives are responsible for certain kinds of behavior, because motives are hypothetical constructs which cannot be seen, handled, smelled, or otherwise tangibly observed. One of the approaches in motivation research is to ask consumers to describe their feelings about products in such a way that ultimate motives and values come out.[27] Thus, researchers usually rely on a combination of various qualitative research techniques to try to establish the presence and/or the strength of various motives.[28]

Behaviors

Since counterfeiting is generally illegal worldwide, the behavior of buyers is surely different from that of consumers who go to official luxury outlets. Another approach to studying the needs-goals paradigm is the means-end analysis.[29] Values influence attitudes which, in turn, influence behavior. However, this approach was not adopted in our study because the key point here was to understand the buyers' motivations and needs rather than their value systems: we were not setting out to judge the morality of their behavior.

Analysis of the research conducted in China, Japan, and Europe revealed eight profiles of luxury counterfeit buyers whose primary motivation was, to varying degrees, one of price: the counterfeits were cheaper than the originals. This was the first step in their purchasing process. The eight categories are set out below.

The tourist

The tourist is typically someone who buys a counterfeit luxury product on their travels. They can be one-time buyers to regular shoppers—a mum who buys a fake Chanel bag for her daughter to a flight attendant who knows "all the best places" in Asia to buy high-quality counterfeits of any brand. The tourist consumer will buy counterfeits for herself or for someone in her immediate circle as a souvenir, though some may not ever use the product back home because she would feel embarrassed if someone noticed it was a fake.

The rationalist

The rationalist is a consumer who refuses to pay a high price for a product she thinks is not "worth" it, believing the high price to reflect the marketing costs rather than the actual cost of the product. Therefore luxury goods are not "worth" more in quality and value than the counterfeits. This type of buyer is very rational in her purchasing decision-making and believes she can "see" the real value of goods in general.

The show-off

The show-off buys counterfeited goods bearing the iconic logos and trademarks of the genuine brands. What show-offs are looking for is the immediate recognition by others of the brand they carry. They want to make sure everyone knows they have the trendy brand of the moment. Most will attempt to convince others they have the genuine brands. These "publicly self-conscious consumers"[30] are driven by how others perceive them. They buy well-known brands (albeit fake) to convey social status and image to others.

The imitator

The imitator buys luxury counterfeits to copy their celebrity idols (a pop-star or a famous actress, for example) or a group of people of a social class to which they know they will never belong. For instance, an employee working in a luxury hotel who sees hotel guests with bags that often cost more than her monthly salary may choose to buy a good-quality counterfeit bag so she can "be like them."

The conformist

The conformist buys luxury counterfeits to fit in with and, more importantly, be accepted by her social group. An example often cited was that of a consumer who would feel obliged to buy a brand that every other member of her group had. If she couldn't afford to buy the genuine brand, she chose a good-quality counterfeit and was constantly scared of the day someone would realize it was a fake.

The hedonist

The hedonist buys genuine brands as well as counterfeits, depending on her mood and often for her own instant pleasure. This type of buyer consumes for her own pleasure and enjoys the opportunity to "fool" her entourage. She is often able to get away with the counterfeit products because her entourage rarely knows which is fake and which is not. Examples ranged from a diamond dealer who owned a pair of fake diamond earrings to someone who bought a jumper of a genuine brand and another color in a counterfeit so she could wear them alternately.

The fooled

The fooled consumer buys counterfeits by mistake. She may buy it from Internet auction sites (such as e-Bay) or from an unauthorized dealer without knowing it. Uneducated luxury consumers often do not know that luxury brands in most countries distribute their goods only to authorized dealers. In countries where such a system is not reinforced by the law, opportunities arise for unauthorized dealers to set up "multi-brand" shops and sell counterfeits.

The rebel

The rebel purchases counterfeits to protest against the dominance of established brands that often care only about their profits. Rebels refuse to contribute to the growth of the genuine brands. They may also buy counterfeits just because they are illegal. Some respondents reported to being "thrilled" by the experience of buying illicit products and bringing them home through customs. This result is consistent with other studies which found that consumers' willingness to purchase counterfeit goods (not specifically luxury counterfeits) was related to their attitudes toward lawfulness.[31]

The study revealed that there is a high concentration of show-offs and imitators in the Chinese luxury market.[32] The more conspicuous Chinese luxury consumers become "idols" for young office workers and students to imitate. As with their Japanese counterparts, while Chinese counterfeit buyers like luxury goods and are very familiar with the brands, their limited budgets mean they cannot afford originals. Buying a high-quality counterfeit is an alternative for them to achieve their dream and to enjoy the happiness that comes from possessing—and being seen to possess—a revered product.

Because counterfeit luxury products can be found in every major Chinese city, unlike their European and Japanese counterparts, Chinese buyers don't need to travel to find what they want. Such has been the incredible improvement in the quality of counterfeit products that some hedonistic Chinese buyers have become specialists in, and regular buyers of, the fakes. Although they may enjoy high social status and be regular consumers of genuine luxury products, they also enjoy the process of discovery, judgment, and assessment of superior-quality counterfeits that can be mixed with their original luxury products.

From unfulfilled need to final purchase

After analyzing and comparing the results of the studies across three countries (China, Japan, and France), we concluded that the main motivations for purchasing counterfeits were similar in each. Although each country had its own specialties, the eight identified motivations were stable and consistent. Based on this, we were able to classify unfulfilled needs as social needs, personal needs, and functional needs for the counterfeits. The principal social motivation of those such as the imitators, for example, who couldn't afford genuine luxury goods, was of wanting to be like those who could afford such things. The needs of the show-off and the conformist were also socially motivated by an inability to buy the genuine article and yet being pushed by their social environment to have the next best thing—the counterfeit version. It is through counterfeit products that they were able to have their various social needs met.

Into the category of fulfilling personal needs comes the rebel, whose opposition to the idea of luxury and luxury brands is manifest in a deliberate decision to favor the counterfeit over the original. For the hedonist, the personal need takes the form of the fun to be had from the process of finding super-quality counterfeits.

The needs of the rational buyer of counterfeits are functional. Their interest lies in the area of the design and the value for money offered by the counterfeits. If the products are well-designed copies of the originals, of superior quality, and offered at mass-market prices, the rational buyer becomes a repeat buyer, loyal to the products and the underground stores where they are sold.

It is clear from this that there are two fundamentally different kinds of behavior in evidence here: there is a deliberate seeking out of counterfeits with a view to purchase, and there is the casual purchase which just happens when the occasion arises. In the first, there is a strong element of deliberate repeat purchase: the buyers are regular and loyal consumers of counterfeit products. In the second, the behavior is more occasional rather than loyal and regular.

Just as luxury consumers are segmented into four groups—lovers, intellectuals, followers, and laggards—so too may buyers of counterfeit luxury goods be classified into three groups, which we call non-consumers, potential luxury consumers, and potential counterfeit consumers, as set out in Figure 5.7.

FIGURE 5.8: *Motivations for buying luxury counterfeits*

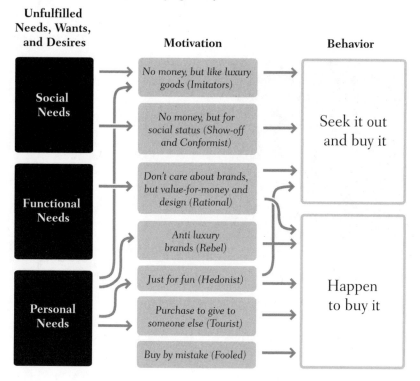

The hedonist, the tourist, and the fooled are occasional counterfeit buyers and thus fall within the mixed area between counterfeit buyers and luxury consumers; we refer to them as potential counterfeit consumers.

The imitator, the show-off, and the conformist buy counterfeits as a way of pursuing luxury brands and a luxury lifestyle within their limited financial means. Although they are loyal buyers of counterfeits, they would undoubtedly become luxury consumers if their financial situation improved. These are the potential luxury consumers.

Finally, irrespective of their financial ability to buy luxury products, the rebel and the rationalist oppose luxury products and would not buy them under any circumstances as a matter of principle.

From the perspective of the luxury brands, it is only right that they should take strong legal action to uphold intellectual property rights and

FIGURE 5.9: *Luxury counterfeit market and luxury consumer market*

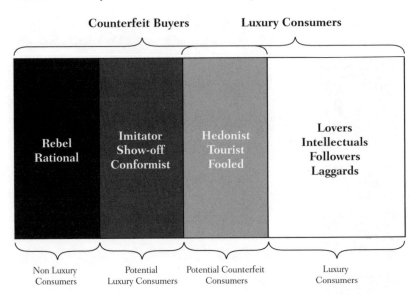

to protect themselves against counterfeiting activities. On the other hand, from a marketing viewpoint, many current counterfeit buyers are potential consumers of genuine luxury brands and it is therefore important that the luxury brands pay more attention to educating these potential consumers, orienting them away from the fakes and toward a greater respect for the creativity of talented designers and their work.

ENDNOTES

1   Goldsmith Ronald E. and Charles F. Hofacker, 1991, "Measuring Consumer Innovativeness", *Journal of the Academy of Marketing Science*, Vol. 19 (summer).

2   Schiffman and Kanuk, 2000, *Consumer Behavior*, seventh edition, Prentice Hall, Inc. and Tsinghua University Press.

3   Schütte, 2000, *Consumer Behavior in Asia*, Macmillan.

4   Rogers, E.M., 1983, *Diffusion of Innovations*, New York: The Free Press; Kotler, P. and Keller, K.L., 2007, *A Framework for Marketing Management*, third edition, New Jersey.

5   Le Nagard-Assayag and Pras, 2003, "Innovation et Marketing Strategique", in Muster and Penan (eds.) *Encyclopédie de l'innovation*, Paris, Economica.

6   Putrevu and Kenneth, 1994, "Comparative and noncomparative advertising: Attitudinal effects under cognitive and affective…", *Journal of Advertising*, Vol. 23 Issue 2; Mittal, 1994, "A study of the concept of affective choice mode for consumer decisions", *Advances in Consumer Research*, Vol. 21, Issue 1.

7   Schiffman and Kanuk, op. cit.

8   See Leslie Cole and Dan Sherrell, 1995, "Comparing Scales to Measure Compulsive Buying: An Exploration of. Their Dimensionality", *Advances in Consumer Behaviors*.

9   Festinger, Leon, 1957, *A Theory of Cognitive Dissonance*, Stanford, CA: Stanford University Press.

10 Schiffman and Kanuk, op. cit.

11 Ibid.

12 Ibid.

13 Ibid.

14 In conversation with the author.

15 In conversation with the author.

16 In conversation with the author.

17 In conversation with the author.

18 In conversation with the author.

19 Bamossy, Gary and Debra L. Scammon, 1985, "Product Counterfeiting: Consumers and Manufacturers Beware", in *Advances in Consumer Research*, 12: pp. 334–9.

20 Chakraborty, Goutam, Anthony Allred, Ajay Singh Sukhdial, and Terry Bristol, 1997, "Use of Negative Cues to Reduce Demand for Counterfeited Products", *Advances in Consumer Research*, Vol. 24, pp. 435–49.

21 Ibison, David, "Luxury fakes cost makers $4.3bn a year", *Financial Times*, FT.com site, 17 January 2006.

22 *The Economic Effect of Counterfeiting and Piracy*, OECD, Paris, 2007.

23 Cordell, Victor V., Nittaya Wongtada and Robert L. Kieschnick Jr., 1996, "Counterfeit Purchase Intentions: Role of Lawfulness Attitudes and Product Traits as Determinants", *Journal of Business Research*, Vol. 35, pp. 41–53.

24 Nia, Arghavan and Judith Lynne Zaichkowsky, 2000, "Do counterfeits devalue the ownership of luxury brands?", *Journal of Product and Brand Management*, Vol. 9, Issue 7, p. 485.

25 Bamossy and Scammon, op. cit.

26 Schiffman and Kanuk, op. cit., p. 64.

27 Dugree, Jeffrey F. et al., 1996, "Observations: Translating Values into Product Wants", *Journal of Advertising Research*, 36(6), pp. 90–9.

28 Belk, Russell et al., 1996, "Metaphors of Consumer Desire," *Advances in Consumer Research*, 23: pp. 368–73.

29 Gutman, Jonathon, 1982, "A Means-End Chain Model Based on Consumer Categorization Processes", *Journal of Marketing*, 46: pp.60–72.

30 Bushman, Brad J., 1993, "What's in a Name? The Moderating Role of Public Self-Consciousness on the Relation between Brand Label and Brand Preference", *Journal of Applied Psychology*, Vol. 78, Issue 5, pp. 857–61.

31 See, for example, Cordell, et al, 1996.

32 Xiao Lu, Pierre and Bernard Pras, 2006, "Une typologie des consommateurs de produits de luxe en Chine", in *La Chine dans la mondialisation, Marché et Stratégies*, Ed. Philippe Béraud, Maisonneuve et Larose Edition, Paris.

CHAPTER 6

Opportunities for Chinese Luxury Brands

Among the factors for victory, to act in accordance with astrological rules is not as important as to choose a favorable direction to array the troops, and to choose a favorable direction to array the troops is not as important as the unity of the generals and the soldiers.
Mencius (371–289 B.C.)

A FTER 30 YEARS of stability and rapid economic development, the Chinese market is ready to accept all kinds of high-end products, and consumers are thirsty for every kind of luxury product. This is a wonderful time for designers and businessmen to create Chinese luxury brands.

Three strategies to develop a Chinese luxury brand

To create a brand is hard; to create a luxury brand is very hard; and to create a luxury brand in China is extremely hard. In financial markets, the rule is "high risk, high gain." In the current luxury market, however, it is not a problem of high risk but of high difficulty in finding the key components to create a Chinese luxury brand: no world-class designers, no long brand histories, and no legendary stories. If these basic conditions can be fulfilled, the high return can be assured.

Strategy # 1: Buy a brand, buy a story

Story, history, and heritage are the essence of a luxury brand. They are the key attributes for a luxury product and also some of the most valuable for clients to consume and to enjoy.

In China, there are brands with a very long history. In Beijing, for example, there are Ruifuxiang (瑞蚨祥), Buyingzhai (步赢斋), and Tongshenghe (同升和) in the traditional couture field. But they are still traditional workshops, lacking industrial reforms and without a modern management system. They are state-owned brands, symbols of traditional Chinese craftsmanship. They represent more than social and cultural capital but they are not market-driven and their management teams do not know how to get the maximum benefit from these valuable entities.

So, for a businessman who wants to do luxury business in China the only solution is to acquire an international brand and adapt it to the Chinese market. This is not as difficult as it may at first sound. In the world market, there are many medium or famous brands in difficulty. Some may have had high brand awareness and considerable value but they also had colossal debts which have allowed them to be bought for as little as US$1. In the 1990s, Asian entrepreneurs, notably Japanese businessmen, bought French luxury brands. But these all ended in failure. Recently, Dickson Poon, the powerful Hong Kong luxury products distributor, bought S.T. Dupont; Lee Ka Shing, Hong Kong's richest man, bought the European perfume retailing chain Marionaud; and Madame Wang, from Taiwan, bought Lanvin.

Owning a world-famous luxury brand is one thing; making it profitable is quite another. This strategy has three basic premises: having sufficient capital to acquire a problem brand and handle any debts it may have; having an experienced international management team with the ability to ensure a smooth handover and a successful turnaround; and having a successful business model and realizable business plan to guide the acquisition.

Acquiring and turning around a failing international brand requires a heavy financial investment. It is not about margins, but how to sell a strong brand identity at full price. This industry is very different from mass-market industries and needs a management team that knows the luxury business inside out: from production and logistics systems to marketing and communications to retailing and financial systems. The third factor in all of this, a proven and realizable business model for the Chinese market, is summarized in Figure 6.1:

FIGURE 6.1: *Business model for luxury business in China*

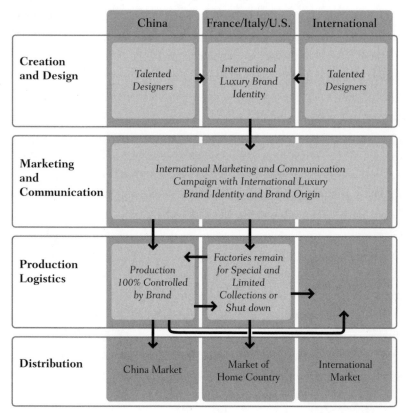

The essence of this model is that it retains the international brand identity while production facilities are transferred to Mainland China to take advantage of cost reductions and to boost margins.

In acquiring the brand—complete with story and image—you should also ensure that you keep the designers and marketing and communication teams. Any cost cutting should be in production and logistics, not in creation, design, and communication. This is the core of your competitive advantage in the China market.

Production costs in Europe and North America are very high, even with luxury products. To reduce costs while maintaining the same level of quality means opening factories in China, limiting your European or U.S. activities to sampling, prototyping, and quality control. Having 100%-controlled factories in China ensures that craftsmanship know-how remains within the company. At the same time, you take advantage of low production costs while maintaining total quality control. Being positioned inside such a potentially vast luxury market relieves you of the burden of import duties, which for luxury goods have been known to double overnight. These savings can then be reinvested in new product designs and new technologies.

The one possible issue that can be raised as a potential drawback to this plan is the question of perceptions regarding the country of origin of your products. You cannot avoid these questions, but the solution is quite simple: in your brand communication, focus more on the international brand image and aesthetic designs, rather than on the Chinese origin, of your products. Let silence and time prove the quality and service of your product offerings.

The key is to sell at international prices, in China and on the international market, while manufacturing the products in China. With this model, you can maintain the highest margins in the world of fashion industry while keeping the lowest production costs. This is also the secret of Ports International's success in the Chinese fashion and luxury market, as outlined in the case study below.

* * *

CASE STUDY

PORTS INTERNATIONAL AND PORTS 1961

Pioneering and pricing advantages help Ports Design outmaneuver global luxury giants in a burgeoning market[1]

COPIES OF *Le Monde* and photos of bleached-blonde Western beauties accent the window displays at Ports 1961, one of the dozens of luxury fashion stops in and around Xintiandi, a premier shopping area in Shanghai. Inside, deep wooden shelves, a high ceiling, and soft tones create a relaxed atmosphere. At hundreds of dollars a piece, the selection of women's business suits and skirts is priced like imported European labels such as Anteprima and Max Mara.

Yet the less celebrated Ports Design is a Sino-Canadian company. Unlike most luxury fashion items sold in China, its goods are manufactured domestically. The combination of thriving Chinese sales, well-crafted designs, good fabrics, and low manufacturing costs explains how the 45-year-old brand is today one of the most profitable in the global fashion industry. Ports this year makes it to *Forbes'* list of Best Under a Billion businesses in Asia-Pacific.

Behind its rise is Alfred Chan, the lanky 59-year-old cofounder and chief executive who shuttles among Ports offices in China, New York, and Toronto. (His partner and brother, Edward, 64, helps to set strategy but isn't involved in running the business.) Chan predicts same-store sales at free-standing shops like the one at Xintiandi—part of a network of 330 Ports boutiques in China—will grow at a double-digit pace annually for years. Sales will also grow as the company fans out to regional capitals to reach a new generation of well-off shoppers, as incomes in China rise and fashion buyers become savvier.

"Ports has an international image, even though the products are made in China" and the Chans were born in Xiamen in Fujian province, says Fanny Lu, the fashion managing editor at the Chinese-language edition of *Vogue* magazine. "The quality," she says, "is actually very good, and they should continue to do well" by targeting women professionals or managers who are receptive to the cosmopolitan message.

With sales of barely $100 million a year (86% in China), Ports faces larger global brands. Yet Chan sees that gap as less of a handicap than an indicator of how large Ports can eventually grow. "If you believe that the Chinese market will be the same size as the U.S. market, we are going to do well," he says. That optimism is apparent among Ports shareholders, too. The company's Hong Kong-traded shares have increased 30% in the past year, versus 15% for the exchange's main index.

The Chan family's success has not come overnight. They moved to Hong Kong from China in 1954 after the Communist takeover and eventually immigrated to Canada, seeking a fortune in the textile trade—enticed, like many from Hong Kong, by incentives for entrepreneurs. Son Alfred graduated from Montreal's McGill University with a physics degree but went back into textiles. Edward joined the family business early on and didn't go to university. The clan owned a factory in China and also imports goods for retail at North American chains.

One of those was Ports International, which had 50 outlets, including a flagship at Fifth Avenue and 57th Street in Manhattan.

In 1989 the family got hold of Ports from its retiring founder. But soon a global recession pinched apparel. The Chans mostly exited the holding company for Ports, and the brand fell into creditors' hands. Stock investors lost money, and the family's reputation was damaged.

Yet, like many of Asia's tycoons (their 46% stake in Ports is worth $442 million), the brothers Chan bounced back from adversity. They decided to focus on the Asian turf and bought back the marketing rights for Ports in the region in 1993 (the global rights came in 1995). Changing the brand to Ports 1961 (which signifies the year it was founded), they zeroed in on China, encouraged, in part, by an optimistic report from Alfred, who had gone to look over the operations of two early Ports shops in Beijing and Xiamen.

"We had read all of that data about Chinese people having low per capita income, but the statistics in our own stores were telling a different story—we were doing better than expected," he says. "After three months I went back to Toronto and I told my family that we have to take the Chinese situation very seriously because of the improvements in income." By going in, the company would also gain first-mover advantage. Today no other luxury retail chain has even a quarter as many China stores.

But getting in early took imagination. Today's glittering luxury shopping districts like Xintiandi not long ago had run-down structures unattended during the decades of the Mao-era chaos. Consumers were still isolated from global style currents.

"For fashion companies, it is all about anticipating the needs of consumers and fulfilling that need," Chan says. "So we early on spent a lot of time educating the consumer about wardrobe investment and explaining that, if you want to be taken seriously, you have to make a certain amount of investment in your wardrobe. They didn't really understand that."

Ports and the Chans took on a continuing problem for foreign companies in China: staffing. To run even its flagship stores, Ports didn't send in hot-shots from New York, its most influential market. (It maintains a design showroom in Manhattan's hot Chelsea district and sells at Saks Fifth Avenue.) Instead, it moved in Chinese speakers experienced in retail from immigrant-rich Toronto and Vancouver.

Strategy # 2: Create your brand, sell it big

With a Chinese fashion market and the cultural elements in place, this is a perfect situation for both designers and businessmen to develop a Chinese fashion and luxury brand. From a venture capitalist's point of view, these two elements perfectly fulfill the basic conditions for a successful project. Thus the second strategy is to create a brand and sell it big.

Obviously the first requirement is for a talented designer to create collections that combine modernity and international vision with traditional Chinese elements; one who is capable of fusing traditional and post-modern influences in a way that will satisfy both modern Chinese consumers and international clients. Finding such a person will not be an easy task but it is an essential pre-condition.

Once this has been done, the next step is to launch collections through fashion shows in international fashion weeks and begin to build brand awareness through opening the first boutique in a strategic location. Very often, designers start their careers by working for established designers or brands. Before launching new collections under their own name, they will already have built some awareness or achievements in the market. Any new designer or brand should be attuned to the fashion cycle and have continuous launches to build awareness through the fashion media. Marc Jacobs started work for Louis Vuitton on condition that LVMH would help him launch a fashion luxury brand under his own name.

The location of the first boutique is crucial. Ideally, this would be in one of the Asian luxury fashion centers such as Hong Kong, Singapore, or Shanghai. This is exactly what David Tang Wing-Cheung did in 1994 when he launched Shanghai Tang in Hong Kong, the perfect place to mix East and West. Ports International chose Shanghai and Xiamen to begin their ventures in the Chinese market, strategic locations that guarantee high brand visibility and attract high-end customers.

All these marketing and retailing measures (fashion shows and communication, boutiques and decoration, sales and management team, production and logistics ...) are expensive, especially when at least two fashion shows per year—possibly in different parts of the world simultaneously—are needed to alert the media and the public to each season's new collection. And this even before the brand starts to earn any money. For many new fashion brands with high potential but limited capital, the best strategy is to join one of the bigger luxury groups which can offer the necessary capital support, retailing networks, management team, and international markets.

Such an alliance between new fashion brands and international fashion and luxury groups is one way for Chinese brands to gain immediate international exposure, as the following case study illustrates.

CASE STUDY

SHANGHAI TANG

The leading edge of modern Chinese chic[2]

SHANGHAI TANG, founded in 1994 by Hong Kong businessman David Tang Wing-Cheung, was acquired four years later by the Swiss-based Richemont Group, the world's second-largest luxury company. The name "Shanghai Tang" evokes the elegance and charm of fashionable Shanghai in the 1930s, when the city was renowned as "the Paris of the East" or, less charitably, as "the whore of the Orient."

At the dawn of the 21st century, the eyes of the world are riveted on China as the ancient nation embarks on a path of unrivalled economic growth, unmatched modernization, and phenomenal projects on a world-beating scale. While the West looks toward China, anxious not to miss the consumerist train as it finally pulls out of the station, Shanghai Tang has departed on its own conquest of fashion all over the world. Its message is unique and remarkable: Shanghai Tang creates luxurious, modern Chinese chic with themes deeply rooted in ancient and authentic Chinese culture, from calligraphy to Peking Opera to Chinese contemporary art. According to its founder, "Shanghai Tang is the best of 5,000 years of Chinese tradition exploding into the 21st Century."

Following the acquisition by Richemont, Shanghai Tang has gradually embarked on the road of the world's top brands. Under its current executive chairman, Raphael Le Masne, it has developed a world-class luxury positioning, revitalizing Chinese design by interweaving it with the dynamism of the 21st century, producing a vibrant and witty fusion of "East meets West."

At its inception in 1994, Shanghai Tang's Hong Kong boutique attracted over one million visitors. By the year 2000, store visits had surpassed four million. Today, Shanghai Tang is the only Chinese luxury brand: the apogee of the Chinese art of living and creativity. The product offer includes a full range of clothing for men, women, and children, plus home furnishings, accessories, and gifts—all of which enhance the concept of revitalized Chinese arts. Shanghai Tang's products are renowned for combining traditional Chinese design and motifs with tongue-in-cheek humor and a contemporary sensibility.

Unique to Shanghai Tang is Imperial Tailors, which revives the diminishing art of Chinese haute couture—delicately crafted apparel redelivered by a team of traditional Shanghainese tailors. It offers a made-to-measure clothing service in the finest tradition of old-fashioned tailoring, with painstaking attention to detail, craftsmanship, luxurious fabrics, and fit. Lush cut velvets, silk jacquards, chiffon, organza, delicate linens, and printed cottons provide an exciting collection of brilliant colors and textures from which a full range of exclusive designs may be chosen.

Like all the major international brands, Shanghai Tang has flagship boutiques in the shopping capitals of the world. Its global network of boutiques includes Shanghai, New York, Paris, London, Hong Kong, and Singapore, to name a few, offering discerning shoppers a big taste of the Shanghai Tang experience and lifestyle. The one-of-kind shopping experience at Shanghai Tang engages all five senses and brings pleasure and, most importantly, a sense of spontaneity to luxury shopping.

Brand strategy

After the acquisition, the Richemont Group began to target 25- to 50-year-old middle- and high-income earners, people who, according to Raphael Le Masne, "dare to be different, happy to show their personality." On this basis, he said, they imported Western designers to transform the Chinese clothing through absorbing many of the latest international fashion elements. "Our designers from Paris, Rome, London, New York ... fuse fashions of different cultural backgrounds, so our brand's creativity is from both Chinese culture and different cultures from around the world with fresh elements to create a unique personality; that's why we can always come to the fore."

Shanghai Tang's clothing, which can be for special occasions or for more everyday wear, can be mixed with other brands to create a stylish effect.

Differentiation is what gives the brand its competitive edge. To underline this, Raphael Le Masne signed an agreement with the Shaolin Temple which enabled the brand to launch a series of Kung Fu images of Shaolin monks which have won it a loyal following from movie stars such as Leung Jiahui and Cheng Peipei.

To protect the brand image, Shanghai Tang became the first luxury fashion brand accepted by the Chinese Trademark Association.

Marketing events

In the luxury market, where a brand's history and spirit is often more important than the product itself, goods cannot be marketed in the same way as mass-market brands. Most luxury consumers seek elegance and taste from a brand. However, in keeping a low profile they also hope that people can appreciate the underlying meaning of their luxury consumption. Luxury marketing therefore needs to be able to both highlight the user's taste and yet maintain a low profile. This is the so-called low-key luxury, which requires special channels to convey the spirit of the brand without having it depreciated by association with the methods employed by mass-market advertising. Below are some of the more recent approaches to marketing taken by Shanghai Tang.

In October 2007, Shanghai Tang, as a sponsor for the Hong Kong Cancer Fund's breast cancer awareness campaign, offered its limited edition "Pink Revolution" keychain in all of its stores. All profits from the sale of this specially designed item are donated to support the campaign. At the same time, at its London flagship store, Shanghai Tang introduced the "Endless Knot" keychain—a motif chosen because of its association with longevity, strength and integrity—in support of the Breast Cancer Research Fund in Britain.

Inspired, as ever, by the kaleidoscopic traditions and histories behind modern-day China, in 2007, Shanghai Tang chose the Silk Road—synonymous with exoticism, opulence, adventure, and danger—as the theme of its Autumn–Winter ready-to-wear collections.

The fashion show—reproducing landscapes from the fabled Silk Road—created stunning visual effects complemented by exquisite chocolate bonbons with similarly evocative flavors such as sesame, chili, ginger, Turkish delight, and sea-salt caramel.

In keeping with the theme, the collection drew on a diverse range of inspirations, from different peoples and eras in the history of the Silk Road. Many of the prints combined tribal Central Asian motifs with more familiar Han Chinese elements. The collection featured luxuriant suede and leathers, embellished with studs and jade, evoking the nomadic lifestyle, where wealth and luxury were literally worn on the sleeve.

In promoting its brand, Shanghai Tang also collaborates with other famous brands. For example, in the summer of 2007, it launched the third installment of its design collaboration with Puma, the sporting goods brand, combining instantly recognizable features of both brands into a unique and eye-catching sports shoe.

Special social campaign

In April 2007, Shanghai Tang inaugurated the Mandarin Collar Society, championing a modern, chic alternative to the traditional necktie. Describing this new venture as "an elegant Chinese-inspired style for men," Raphael Le Masne sees it as a demonstration that China "is more than the world's factory. Today, we demonstrate that China can also make a difference in the fashion scene, proposing a stylish way to dress in today's world of individualism and comfort."

This slightly cheeky initiative brings together prominent men in diverse fields, such as sports, business, politics, and the arts, appointing MCS Ambassadors including British sprint champion Linford Christie, Michelin star chef Pierre Gagnaire, Shanghai Tang founder David Tang, and Shui On chairman Vincent Lo Hong-sui. Initially, Shanghai Tang will invite 88 members only (eight ambassadors and 80 members), who will be granted exclusive access to made-to-measure merchandise on a bi-monthly basis and an impeccable follow-up service at Shanghai Tang flagships in Hong Kong, New York, London, and Singapore.

Conclusion

Without doubt, China represents the biggest growth market for luxury goods, with an expected growth to 2015 of 108%. In the process, it is predicted to become the world's largest consumer of luxury goods by 2011. Shanghai Tang's birth and development onto the world stage may be regarded as a start for China's domestic luxury industry. The reasons for Shanghai Tang's success are clear: first is the brand's individual style, which relies on strong Chinese characteristics; second is the role the company plays as a cultural interpreter within China's history; and last, but by no means least, is the superb brand management and operational skills brought to the brand by Richemont. Perhaps as *BusinessWeek* has predicted, Shanghai Tang will become China's Chanel.

Strategy #3: Create your brand, build your own legend

The third strategy to develop a Chinese luxury brand is the most difficult but the most valuable. It is also a duplication of the history of luxury houses such as Hermès and Louis Vuitton in France, Gucci and Prada in Italy, Burberry and Dunhill in the U.K., Breguet and Patek Philippe in Switzerland, and Coach in the U.S. In the vast majority of these cases, success began with craftsmanship with deep cultural roots. After several generations of effort, they were accepted as luxury brands in their respective home countries. Each had a strong cultural identity and came to be seen as a symbol, as the cultural capital of the country.

For a new Chinese fashion brand to become a real luxury brand using this strategy requires a lot of hard work, talent and patience, and a great deal of courage on the part of the designer. Currently, there is only one company in the Chinese market which has adopted this toughest of all approaches: NE Tiger.

* * *

Top Chinese Fashion Brand[3]

AS CHINA experiences robust economic growth and its citizens become increasingly affluent, the Chinese luxury product market is set to gain a significant market share. NE Tiger, Mainland China's first luxury brand, aims to gain a foothold in this expanding industry. While NE Tiger should be applauded for its brave efforts and strong vision, its branding efforts are still insufficient for the brand to meet its goals.

Background

The "NE Tiger" brand name was registered in 1992 by Zhang Zhifeng, a Heilongjiang native born to a family of tailors. He followed the family trade and started out as a tailor, occasionally dabbling in garment design before moving on to the manufacture, design, and distribution of clothing. As a young man, Zhang spent his days frequently traveling between Heilongjiang, Shanghai, and other parts of China. He firmly believed that fur and skins were the epitome of wealth and affluence and that they would be a perfect representation of luxury.

On a visit to New York in 1988, Zhang was struck by the sheer size of the luxury goods market. He passionately believed that China needed to have its own luxury brand. On his return to China, he began consolidating his resources and moved toward building a luxury goods brand, opening design centers in New York, Paris, and Milan in an attempt to gain a foothold in the fashion industry.

Zhang noticed that the history of luxury goods in the West stemmed back to Europe's feudal and aristocratic days and he firmly believed that China's 5,000 years of civilization provided enough historical legitimacy to be just as able to give luxury goods consumers in China the same feeling of class and affluence. Thus, NE Tiger's designs mostly boast a Chinese theme or feel.

To ensure his products were of the best quality, Zhang used stringent quality controls, putting his skins through more than 120 checks. Currently, NE Tiger gets its skins from animals reared under strictly controlled environments in Nordic Europe. In 2000, NE Tiger joined the largest fur provider and auction house, Kopenhagen Fur's Purple Club, giving him greater access to top-quality skins supplied only to top international brands.

NE Tiger's success so far can be attributed primarily to Zhang's acute business sense and charisma. As a brand choosing to capitalize on China's rich history and culture, NE Tiger also plays toward Chinese nationalism. However, NE Tiger had to create a buzz of excitement around its products and incorporate them into a lifestyle, a culture that would resonate well with its target clientele.

Brand building

Branding is a widely misunderstood term and is often used interchangeably with "marketing." However, branding encompasses much more than mere marketing and includes everything from strategy to communication to talent attraction and retention. A strong brand is a signal of quality and consumers associate themselves with the values and attributes behind it.

Zhang soon realized the immense value that a strong brand could add to products and decided to start building up his own brand name. He stopped production of low-end garments, consolidated his resources by selling off unrelated assets and used these resources to break into the high-end fashion market. He was convinced that product, branding, and reputation were the three key factors to ensuring NE Tiger's success.

NE Tiger has 5,000 years of Chinese culture and civilization firmly entrenched in its brand promise. As Zhang puts it, "Fashion has no borders, but brands need roots. Luxury goods brands require history and culture." NE Tiger is thus identified and positioned as a luxury brand by China for China and, eventually, the world. NE Tiger based its brand on its fur products, which Zhang believes to be the ultimate luxury.

NE Tiger hopes that its customers will be drawn away from Western cultures of luxury and return to their Chinese roots. Zhang believes that China has as much to offer as the West; all it requires is to fill the gaps left by the Cultural Revolution.

Strengths, weaknesses, and solutions

As a new entrant into the luxury goods industry and a brand with only 15 years of history, NE Tiger is faced with the mammoth task of breaking into a market where history and culture play an extremely important role in determining the health of a brand. Yet, because of its youth and other external factors which we will look into later, NE Tiger has been able to develop in ways that its competitors could not have dreamed of when they first started out.

The Chinese luxury market generates more than US$20 billion a year in sales[4] and is expected to grow 10% to 20% annually until 2015. By 2010, a quarter of a billion consumers in China will be able to afford luxury goods. Currently, 200 million Chinese consumers can afford a variety of luxury brands; of these, an estimated 50 million are active purchasers of luxury goods.[5]

According to Zhang, luxury goods consumers in China fall into four categories: the blue-blooded aristocrats, the corporate elite, the middle class, and the "dreamy class" or the group of people who use luxury goods as a means of bridging the gap between their dream life and reality. NE Tiger, however, has its sights set on members of the corporate and social elite and white-collar workers as its target clientele. Ernst and Young adds another category to this list: "crowd-averse wealthy consumers who seek personalized services and frequently visit luxury retail outlets for the newest and most fashionable product offerings—without concern for price" are also part of the mix.[6] Others have noted that Asian demand for luxury goods includes a wide range of consumer items and these items are purchased even if the purchasers may not have secured adequate food, clothing, and shelter.[7]

Chinese consumers tend to be less discreet when it comes to purchasing luxury products and most of the time these purchases are meant to distinguish them from the masses and to impress people around them. Unlike their counterparts in India and other developed markets, who are very discerning buyers and extremely conscious of style and fashion, Chinese consumers are usually unaware of the true quality of the products. NE Tiger's clothing will be able to tap into this trend as it is as eye-catching as Versace logos. Also, fur skins have long been a symbol of wealth and affluence. However, this short-term gain will eventually prove detrimental to NE Tiger's long-term development strategy as the latter desperately needs its consumers to carry its products off with the style and ease that discerning buyers have or it will end up as a mere symbolic replacement for cold, hard cash rather than the timeless classic that it strives to become.

As Chinese consumers relate name brands to face, NE Tiger should first and foremost emphasize the distinguished social status of its products in its marketing efforts. Also, as Chinese consumers are more likely to be influenced by their group members in their face consumption,[8] NE Tiger should use word-of-mouth marketing strategies.

As the figure below illustrates, Maslow's hierarchy of needs finds a different expression in Eastern cultures and, given that Chinese consumers are so different from their Western counterparts, NE

Tiger should consider segmenting its garments under different sub-brands to cater to different tastes or, at the very least, use widely different marketing strategies when reaching out to the two different consumer groups

Maslow's hierarchy of needs and the Asian equivalent

Upper-Level Needs	**WEST**	**EAST**
	Self-actualization	Status
	Prestige	Admiration
	Belonging	Affiliation
	Safety	Safety
Lower-Level Needs	Physiological	Physiological

Source: Schütte with Ciarlante 1998.[9]

Brand strategy and communication

NE Tiger has adopted an organic growth strategy, choosing to develop on its own. At present, as a relatively new brand, it is difficult for NE Tiger to compete with long-established and dominant players such as Louis Vuitton, Chanel, and Gucci, which boast the historical legitimacy crucial to the success of luxury products.

Fashion is not about utility; rather, it is a representation of values, attributes, and a lifestyle. Therefore, when branding its products, NE Tiger has taken care to use the most creative and attention-grabbing methods. In 2003, it carried out a "show box" event where models wearing NE Tiger garments were placed in a semi-opaque box with holes at different spots for customers to look through.

In 2002, Zhang began organizing and sponsoring high-brow social events with the aim of cultivating a "NE Tiger lifestyle" by creating brand recognition and loyalty. By inviting elite personalities and celebrities to the events, the company hoped that consumers would associate success, fame, and glamour with its garments. Also, by inviting society's elite to parties and other social events where "play" is always involved, Zhang cleverly put across the idea that success is easy and the easiest way to emulate one of the successful elite members of society is to dress as they do and gain entry into events that they attend.

Through sponsorship of events such as the Asia Super Model contest, indirect alliances with Tsinghua University's Kopenhagen Fur Design Institute, and participation in luxury goods exhibitions, NE Tiger is slowly building up its market presence. As the first Chinese luxury brand, NE Tiger is able to leverage on the novelty effect and create a new niche market.

NE Tiger set up its design centers in fashion capitals such as New York, Paris, and Hong Kong to create the perception that it is an international brand that is sensitive to global fashion trends. NE Tiger's showroom in Shanghai is three stories high and uses a minimalist design to reflect the luxurious and classy feel that its garments and fur skins give. Unlike the other luxury brands, which choose to locate their boutiques in the prime areas of the CBD, NE Tiger chose to set up shop in a fashion-themed business park in faraway Changning district. Although the company is able to save on rent and occupy a larger area in Changning than it would have been able to in the CBD, the lackluster location fails to heighten the sense of exclusivity and affluence for the consumer.

At present, NE Tiger has already captured more than half of the mink-skin market in China and has since diversified its product base to produce evening gowns and wedding gowns as well. Although the Chinese luxury goods market is mostly dominated by foreign players, there are no major players in the niche market that NE Tiger has chosen to enter. In addition, Zhang believes that social events which require the use of exquisite gowns will become increasingly popular as China's economy continues to grow.

1. BRAND AUDIT

Company:
NE Tiger
Owner:
Zhang Zhifeng

Customers
- Newly affluent
- Middle class
- Corporate and social elite
- Global consumers
- Chinese who choose NE Tiger over foreign luxury goods

Competitors
Shanghai Tang, Louis Vuitton, Gucci, Chanel, Fendi etc.

2. BRAND IDENTITY

Brand Vision
- Renaissance and emergence of Chinese luxury goods market
- To showcase Chinese culture through its products to the world

Brand Scope
- Wedding gowns, evening gowns, fur-skin garments

Brand Essence
- Values: Class, Opulence, Nationalism, Success, Fame, Glamour, Freedom
- 5,000 years of civilization captured in a garment

Brand Positioning
- Made by Asians, for Asians
- Inherently Chinese

Brand Personality
- Elegance and Beauty
- Petite and Graceful

3. BRAND STRATEGY

Organic Growth Strategy

4. BRAND IMPLEMENTATION

Customers
- Brand training
- Brand-oriented HR
- Internal communications

External
- MarComm
- Associations and alliances: Kopenhagen Fur, Top Marques
- Exhibitions
- Loyalty club

In order to retain its customers and create a loyal base, NE Tiger has formed its own VIP club, the "NE Tiger fur skin club," which currently has 30,000 members. With so many members, however, it is doubtful whether the club and product can retain their sense of exclusivity.

The enduring success of many long-lasting companies can often be traced back to a visionary individual with the foresight to ensure that the transformation (s)he sets in train can last beyond his/her departure. Zhang is such an individual, with the ability to position NE Tiger as a luxury brand.

In the media, Zhang is often portrayed as a charismatic individual with good business sense, as seen from his initial success in the clothing industry. In his determination to take NE Tiger to the world, he has refused to use distributorships and franchises to gain a foothold in other parts of China, despite having received some 3,000 applications. This has proven to be an intelligent and strategically correct decision as he has elevated NE Tiger to the same theoretical status as foreign luxury brands. He envisions NE Tiger as a timeless, classic brand. By using Chinese culture and history as the main inspiration for its designs, he is able to capture feelings of nationalism in local consumers and use oriental mysticism and its exotic feel to appeal to consumers overseas.

Zhang, as founder, chief designer, and CEO, is the leading ambassador for the NE Tiger brand. Among the audacious goals he has set for it is to make China the "third step of luxury," after Europe and the U.S. Such visionary leaders are what new brands like NE Tiger need to establish their presence.

If there is a blemish in Zhang's otherwise remarkable record, it would be his tendency to come across as flashy and a little theatrical. His public image is of a loud, flamboyant individual always in front of the camera. While CEOs should maintain a regional and international presence to market their brand, it could be argued that Zhang takes this too far for a brand that seeks to position itself as a timeless, classic brand.

NE Tiger's alliances with Kopenhagen Fur and its appearances at several luxury brand exhibitions have certainly helped to elevate its profile. However, should NE Tiger wish to become a truly, world-class brand, it certainly needs to rethink some of its other strategies.

The strongest brands are those which can connect emotionally with their clients: a brand name should be strategic and creative, not functional and descriptive. The name "NE Tiger" (or "Northeast Tiger") combines a direction and an animal; individually and collectively they connote qualities and values which conflict with the values that the brand is trying to portray. For example, "Tiger" brings to mind values of strength, vitality, and masculinity that do not substantiate the ideas of classic timelessness, class, and grace that the brand is trying to personalize. While the brand name might appeal to nationalistic local consumers, it is unlikely that discerning consumers, local and foreign, would take to the product. Furthermore, NE Tiger lacks a striking, easily recognizable corporate logo such as has served Louis Vuitton and Chanel so well.

Currently, 60% of NE Tiger's revenue is generated through OEM (Original Equipment Manufacturer) sales, but plans are in the pipeline to gradually phase these out and replace them with NE Tiger's own products. This strategy is extremely crucial in building up the brand name, especially within local markets. On the other hand, foreign consumers tend to be more discerning shoppers when it comes to luxury products; hence it might be worthwhile for NE Tiger to consider continuing its OEM sales under another sub-brand to break into the foreign markets before introducing its own brand products, by which time they may have matured and would therefore appeal to foreign consumers.

NE Tiger's strategy is to price its products lower than the global average for luxury garments. Luxury products tend to have an upward-sloping demand curve which contributes to their appeal. NE Tiger should consider adjusting its price upward to meet the face-giving needs commonly found in local consumers. Every year, the company launches more than a thousand different designs of gowns and other garments, with each piece not produced more than once or twice. The brand should consider cutting down on its production and, instead, produce selected pieces on a made-to-order basis only. These garments could then be tailored to suit the individual's body shape and tastes.

In a recent Interbrand survey, 66% of respondents believed that the "Made in China" label hurts Chinese brands today. However, modern brands can be nationality-neutral; with a good branding strategy, NE Tiger can overcome negative preconceptions about this label.

The strongest global brands, such as Disney and Nordstrom, have incorporated their brand strategies and values throughout every single level of employment to the extent that employees have their own corporate language. Every employee has to be the central focus and all brand values and strategies have to translate into real life behavior. By understanding the brand vision and the story behind it, employees can come up with new ideas to improve existing processes.

NE Tiger lacks a distinct employee-training and brand-alignment program to ensure that every employee has a clear understanding of what it stands for. In the long run, this would prove to be detrimental to a company whose products need a strong brand more than anything else to thrive.

The company's flagship products are its fur-skin garments and may come under attack as global awareness and sentiment against the use of furs increases. It needs to ensure, therefore, that it uses the most humane methods possible to obtain its raw materials and should, through its engagement in other social-awareness programs, portray itself as a responsible and environmentally concerned company.

Like all other companies, NE Tiger needs to make succession plans for when Zhang steps away from the business. It needs to continually reinvent itself through creating dynamic goals and the best way to do so is to adopt a promote-from-within system to ensure that any successor clearly understands and champions the brand's values.

Shanghai Tang and NE Tiger: A comparison in growth

There are several comparisons that can be drawn between the subjects of our last two cases studies. Shanghai Tang, like NE Tiger, prides itself as a Chinese luxury brand and considers itself the "apogee of the Chinese art of living and Chinese creativity." Its products include clothing for men, women, and children along with accessories, home furnishings, and gifts. It also provides "imperial tailoring" services for customers who prefer to have their outfits customized. Shanghai Tang aims to "create luxurious and modern Chinese chic outfits with themes firmly rooted in Chinese culture." Unlike NE Tiger, Shanghai Tang's designs are a fusion of East and West; it combines Chinese fabric and designs with Western colors and style. When worn by Westerners, the outfits strike others as oriental and stylish. When worn by Chinese, the outfits convey a tinge of Western style, a balance of Chinese and global sensibilities. Shanghai Tang is thus able to suit the tastes of consumers worldwide better than NE Tiger.

In its designs and advertisements, Shanghai Tang portrays the Western values of individualism and freedom strongly. Although the designs are rooted in Chinese culture, they allow for innovation.

For example, its mandarin jackets are reversible and the embroidery can be modified; they don't have to follow strict traditional designs. While Shanghai Tang's designs are made to have Asians looking Western and Westerners looking Asian, NE Tiger's designs aim to have Asians and Westerners alike looking Asian.

Shanghai Tang has a global network of boutiques situated in upmarket shopping centers alongside other luxury brand stores. NE Tiger, on the other hand, has only retail outlets within Mainland China. Shanghai Tang can be said to be a melting pot that brings a global vision to a Chinese context.

While NE Tiger is wholly Chinese-owned, Shanghai Tang is part of the Richemont Group of luxury brands which include Cartier, Mont Blanc, and Piaget amongst others. Shanghai Tang is thus able to capitalize on global marketing strategies but, in doing so, it ceases to be viewed as a home-grown luxury brand.

It is evident, too, that Shanghai Tang's Mandarin Collar Society is very much more successful than NE Tiger's fur-skin club, in positioning, exclusivity, and strategy. Despite entering the market two years later, Shanghai Tang has had greater success in the luxury product market and has been able to establish a presence in the West. Although it labels itself as a luxury brand, it is not as luxurious or exclusive as the other premium brands such as Cartier or Mont Blanc. Thus, NE Tiger still has the opportunity to overtake Shanghai Tang to become the leading Chinese luxury brand. In the long term, NE Tiger will have more room for development, as it is essentially creating a new market space for itself while Shanghai Tang is adapting to existing markets. In a global market where mergers and acquisitions are commonplace, NE Tiger needs to be grounded in its goal to be a purely Chinese, home-grown, luxury brand and ensure that Zhang's successors do not sell off the brand to a foreign company.

According to Interbrand,[10] the primary competitive advantage for most Chinese companies is low-cost manufacturing, leading to low-priced products. As a luxury brand, such a strategy is out of the question for NE Tiger. Rather, the brand has to concentrate on its branding efforts. A top-down initiative, starting from CEO Zhang Zhifeng, is crucial, but NE Tiger has to improve its talent-recruiting efforts in order to have bottom-up support.

NE Tiger's aim to be known across the globe as China's first luxury brand is an ambitious one and will no doubt win the support of native and overseas Chinese. What remains is for the brand to leverage on China's robust economic growth and development and combine trend-setting designs with sound branding strategies to redefine the concept of Chinese fashion and luxury brands.

The ambivalence of the Chinese elite toward Western luxury

When the French luxury lifestyle brand "au nom de la rose" opened its beautiful boutique in Hen Shan Road, the former French concession area in Shanghai, it was very proud of its location and romantic decoration. However, it quickly became apparent to the store's management that attracting Chinese consumers was tough work, despite the fact that the luxury market is booming and the buying power of Chinese consumers is now considerable. The market was there, but still people didn't come into the boutique. Why was this?

The answer is simple: there was a great psychological distance between the luxury boutique and the consumers it sought to attract. Chinese consumers don't feel comfortable going into a French lifestyle luxury product store with a purely French style of decoration. Even Louis Vuitton suffered from the same problem when it first entered the Chinese market in 1992. In fact, it suffered for a very long time without earning money. By enduring, however, it built very high brand awareness such that, by 2005, the positive elements for buying a Louis Vuitton bag finally outweighed all the cultural, social, and economic reasons for not buying. For Louis Vuitton, patience paid dividends.

However, very few new luxury brands can afford to wait 10 years, and have to reach breakeven point as quickly as possible. A basic understanding of the ambivalence of Chinese luxury consumers is necessary if they are to find solutions to this problem.

According to social psychologists this ambivalence consists of two strongly correlated terms: potential ambivalence and felt ambivalence.[11] The degree to which Chinese luxury consumers experience the latter (and thus post-purchase guilt) is dependent on holistic thinking and product category considerations. This will be explained more fully as we go along.

Other social psychology studies have shown that our lives can be rife with cognitive inconsistency; that is, we can display both positive and negative attitudes toward an object at the same time.[12] While most social psychologists are interested in studying attitudinal ambivalence in social and moral issues such as capital punishment or abortion, marketing is interested in attitudinal ambivalence in a specific commercial context by way of solving practical and operational problems when doing business.

In previous chapters, we segmented the Chinese luxury consumer market into four groups (Lovers, Intellectuals, Followers, and Laggards) by using psychographic variables. Here, we explore the differences in attitudinal ambivalence toward luxury consumption between the four groups. In addition, two moderators (Holistic Thinking, and Product Category and Brand Preference Consideration) are used to examine the relation between potential and felt ambivalence. The relations between attitudinal ambivalence and consumer behavior are also analyzed with respect to three consumption characteristics (Innovativeness, Brand Loyalty, and Post-purchase Dissonance).

Attitudinal ambivalence

Of the four approaches to ambivalence—psychological, sociological, cultural, and social-psychological—adopted by psychologists, the fourth is, in our view, the most relevant for studying Chinese luxury consumers.

For psychologists, the term "ambivalence" is used when explaining characteristics of schizophrenia.[13] The "normal" individual feels and lives an "internal experience of mixed emotions" with pleasant and unpleasant feelings experienced simultaneously. This is what is called "psychological ambivalence," which implies in its original definition a simultaneous experience of positive and negative emotions: "acknowledging and resolving mixed feelings are signs of maturity and mental health."[14]

Sociologists, on the other hand, have a broader definition of the construct, arguing that the issue of internal emotional struggle is not the only salient factor to be addressed. The study of ambivalence should also focus on external forces, and on the way the existing social structure can be a source of mixed feelings. Individuals may simultaneously express multiple social roles that are governed by disparate norms. Thus individuals must often reconcile conflicting demands placed on them as they attempt to enact various social roles—each characterized by norms and counter-norms that govern role behavior. When the norms are in conflict, ambivalence often appears. And the more complex the society becomes, the more role conflicts will increase.

The cultural ambivalence approach[15] relies upon conflicts between cultural values. But the differences between the sociological ambivalence, which is based upon conflicting social roles and norms, and cultural ambivalence, with conflicting cultural values, are not very distinct since cultural values are often expressed via social norms.

Some psychologists believe that a potential ambivalence may exist without being strongly felt by the subject, a view that our qualitative study seems to confirm for Chinese consumers of luxury goods.

Social psychologists define attitudinal ambivalence as positive and negative evaluations of an object. A person who has mixed emotions and feels torn about an attitude object feels ambivalent about it.

For our purposes, the social-psychological approach is the most relevant in this special context, since we deal with mixed emotions and feelings toward an object arising from conflicting evolutions in Chinese society. But these social and contradictory evolutions, which can result in potential ambivalence, do not necessarily progress to become felt ambivalence.

Ambivalent attitudes toward luxury goods

In Chapter 4, we saw how there are mixed emotions in Chinese consumers toward their luxury consumption. The attitudinal ambivalence results from conflicting values, processes, or meanings of luxury products in the Chinese cultural context.

As we noted, traditional Chinese values such as economy, frugality, and modesty play a role in forming a negative attitude toward luxury consumption; however, modern and Western values such as the quest for wealth, individualism, and personal freedom generate a positive attitude toward luxury consumption.

Within the consumer process, analysis and impulsiveness are two different and opposing strands co-existing in consumers' minds, defining whether they are analytical (rational) or impulsive (experiential) in their approach and it is interesting to examine if there are correlations between the degree of attitudinal ambivalence and the process differences.

With regard to the meaning of luxury products, the conspicuousness function is the most important motivation for buying luxury goods. However, conspicuousness may decline in importance when excellent quality, avant-garde design, and functional demands are the first priorities for consumers. This is the possible opposition between democratization and elitism. As luxury products always represent a combination of contradictory values and of multiple attributes, even if attitudinal ambivalence exists in consumers' minds, this is very difficult to investigate. Thus, the distinction between potential ambivalence and felt ambivalence is an efficient means of studying non-expressed ambivalence and expressed ambivalence.

Psychographic segmentation of Chinese luxury consumers

The four groups of Chinese luxury consumers mentioned earlier are assumed to have different degrees of ambivalence toward luxury goods. Within the notion of "ambivalence" itself, there are two categories: non-potential and potential. Potential ambivalence that is realized is known as "felt" ambivalence. The degrees to which ambivalence is evident within the various categories is determined by certain moderators, as set out below.

Moderators: Holistic thinking, product category, and brand preference

Holistic thinking

Holistic thought is defined as involving an orientation to the context or field as a whole, including attention to relationships between a focal object and the field, and a preference for explaining and predicting events on the basis of such relationship. Holistic approaches rely on experience-based knowledge rather than on abstract logic and are dialectical, meaning that there is an emphasis on change, recognition of contradiction and of the need for multiple perspectives, and a search for the "Middle Way" between opposing propositions. Holistic thought is associative, and its computations reflect similarity and contiguity.

Analytic thought is defined as involving detachment of the object from its context, a tendency to focus on attributes of the object to assign it to categories, and a preference for using rules about the categories to explain and predict the object's behavior. Inferences rest in part on the practice of decontextualizing structure from content, the use of formal logic, and avoidance of contradiction.[16]

Studies on Chinese values systems show East Asians to be holistic, attending to the entire field and assigning causality to it, making relatively little use of categories and formal logic, and relying on dialectical reasoning, whereas Westerners are more analytic, paying attention primarily to the object and the categories to which it belongs and using rules, including formal logic, to understand behavior.[17]

The Chinese are therefore are able to recognize contradictions easily and do not feel dissonance or discomfort when this occurs. However, the degree of holistic thinking varies from one individual to another and is assumed to change the degree of ambivalence: the person with higher holistic reasoning can accept a contradiction and feel less dissonant or uncomfortable than the person with lower holistic reasoning when confronted with the same contradictory situation.

The product category and brand preference consideration

Previous studies concerning Chinese luxury consumption also show that personal luxury choice is complex and ambivalent. When the product category priority and the brand preference are defined, the attitudes toward the brand and the product become logical and reasonable. The ambivalence therefore decreases.

Attitudinal ambivalence toward luxury changes according to product category consumption priorities and brand consumption preference. The higher the priority accorded to the product categories and brands, the lower the ambivalence amongst the consumers. For example, among the 10 luxury product categories,[18] one respondent's top three priorities may be: first, cosmetics; second, ready-to-wear clothes; and third, leather goods and accessories. This means that the customer will choose more luxury brands in cosmetics than in other product categories, such as gastronomy, and will have fewer ambivalent feelings toward either the consumption of those goods or the goods themselves. When product category priorities are clear and limited, the strong potential ambivalence does not translate into strong felt ambivalence. The same is true when brand preference is clear.

In addition, some other variables may also have a moderating effect. For example, gender influences the order of priorities for product categories. For women, cosmetics are the first product choice; for men, the luxury car is the most important product.

The three consumption characteristic variables presented in Chapter 4—innovativeness, loyalty, and post-purchase guilt—were chosen for this study to examine the relation between felt ambivalence and differences in consumer attitudes and behavior.

Ambivalence and segmentation

An individual belongs to the group with potential ambivalence when his rating does not equal zero; when the rating of an individual equals zero, it means that the individual belongs to the group without potential ambivalence.[19]

FIGURE 6.2: *Attitudinal ambivalence model*[20]

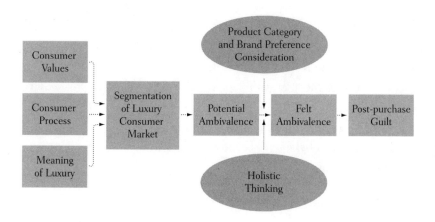

Attitudinal ambivalence

The hypotheses concerning the Chinese luxury consumer's attitudinal ambivalence are confirmed by this study. The strong correlation between potential ambivalence and felt ambivalence toward luxury goods confirmed the conclusion drawn by social psychologists in capital punishment and abortion studies.[21] Potential ambivalence is decided by the individual's value system linked to the specific subject or object. Because ambivalent attitudes arise from values systems which are based on social context and cultural background, these two elements have to be considered in attitudinal ambivalence studies.

This conclusion also confirms our earlier findings concerning Chinese luxury consumer behavior. It again rejects the generalization (exemplified by an article in *The Economist* in 2004[22]) which characterizes Chinese luxury consumer behavior as ostentatious. Such behavior is typical only of certain segments of the total number of consumers in the market, a view confirmed by the psychographic segmentation which shows that the four segments have significant differences in innovativeness, brand loyalty, and post-purchase guilt. The result of the current research is a complementary support to that segmentation and explains Chinese luxury consumer behavior, and especially ambivalence, from a social-psychological viewpoint.

The attitudinal ambivalence of Chinese luxury consumers toward luxury goods explains the diversity of consumer behavior with respect to luxury products, although they have generally a similar social-economic profile. The followers and the laggards are significantly more ambivalent toward luxury goods and luxury consumption than the other two segments. This fact, together with their impulsiveness, leads the followers to suffer the most from post-purchase guilt and inconsistency. On the other hand, the laggards' ambivalent attitude toward luxury goods does not lead to direct post-purchase guilt, because of their strong functionality orientation that motivates luxury buying.

The two moderators

The moderating effects (holistic thinking and product category and brand consideration) decrease the level of ambivalence felt, explaining why Chinese consumers buy luxury goods even though they are potentially ambivalent toward these products. This study confirmed the findings of previous research that Chinese consumers are holistic in their approach to consumption. This has important implications for marketers and their marketing strategies for the Chinese market or markets where Chinese culture is the dominant influence.

The confirmation of the correlation between felt ambivalence and post-purchase guilt shows that inconsistency and dissonance after luxury buying are caused by the consumer's ambivalence. Decreasing the consumer's felt ambivalence toward luxury goods is one way in which the commercial performance of luxury companies in China could be improved. Our study shows that although consumers are potentially ambivalent toward luxury goods, their felt ambivalence can be considerably decreased by their holistic thinking ability and product category and brand considerations.

Post-purchase guilt

Numerous previous studies have focused on post-purchase guilt and proposed different solutions to reduce consumer inconsistency. Our study revealed the cause of post-purchase guilt: the attitudinal ambivalence of the consumers toward luxury goods arising from a diverse and complex array of individual motivations.

We would like to propose two practical solutions for marketers looking to overcome this ambivalence. The first is for the conspicuous and impulsive consumers—the luxury followers. To reduce their felt ambivalence, and thus their post-purchase guilt, the luxury brands should look to enhance their product category and brand considerations that can lead these consumers to a more logical choice of luxury goods. This can be done by helping them choose classical models to increase their brand loyalty and to deepen their understanding of brand and product.

The second proposal concerns the non-conspicuous consumers—the luxury intellectuals and the luxury laggards—whose luxury choices are based more on the functionality of the product and the matching of personal values and brand values, and for whom post-purchase guilt is not as strong. For these consumers, brands should be looking to offer additional services, both during the buying process and through longer-term connections via such things as a brand club or special offers.

For marketers, these two moderators are the key elements to manipulate in their marketing communication and sales activities. Finding reasonable motives for consumers to buy luxury products can help increase their luxury buying while reducing their ambivalence and the possibility of post-purchase guilt. Giving consumers more information about the brand's history and products can also motivate brand loyalty.

ENDNOTES

1   This case study was Russell Flannery's "Tailored for China" cover story of *Forbes Magazine*, 30 November 2006, and is used with permission.

2   This case was written and developed by Zheng Dan, under the author's direction. It is intended to be used as the basis of discussion rather than as a model for handling a management situation. The case was compiled from published sources.

3   This case was written and developed by Lim Huiwen, under the author's direction. It is intended to be used as the basis of discussion rather than as a model for handling a management situation. The case was compiled from published sources.

4   *Shanghai Daily*, 20 May 2005.

5   China Association of Branding Strategy, China Statistics Bureau 2005.

6   *China: The New Lap of Luxury*, Ernst and Young, September 2005.

7   Ram, J., 1994, "Luxury Goods Firms find a haven in Asia", *Asian Business*, Vol. 30, pp. 52–3.

8   "How Face Influences Consumption", *International Journal of Market Research*, Vol. 49, Issue 2.

9   Schütte with Ciarlante, 1998, *Consumer Behaviors in Asia*, New York: University Press.

10   "Made in China: 2007 Brand Study", Interbrand Consulting, 2007.

11   See, for example, Priester and Petty, 1994, "The gradual Threshold Models of Ambivalence: Relating the Positive and Negative Bases of Attitudes to Subjective Ambivalence", *Journal of Personality and Social Psychology*, Vol. 71, Issue 3, p. 431.

12   Newby-Clark, McGregor and Zanna, 2002, "Thinking and Caring about Cognitive Inconsistency: When and For Whom does Attitudinal Ambivalence Feel Uncomfortable?', *Journal of Personality and Social Psychology*, Vol. 82, No. 2, pp. 157–66.

13   Bleuler, E., 1950, *Dementia Praecox or the Group of Schizophrenias*, Zinkin, J, (ed.) New York: International Universities Press.

14   Freud. S., 1965, *The Interpretation of Dreams*, New York: Avalon Books.

15   Hajada, J.,1968, "Ambivalence and Social Relations", *Sociological Focus*, 2 (2): pp. 21–8.

16   Nisbett, Peng, Choi and Norenzayan, 2001, "Culture and systems of thought: Holistic vs. Analytic Cognition", *Psychological Review*, 109: pp. 291–310.

17   Ibid.

18   The 10 luxury product categories are:
     1. Cosmetics and Perfumes
     2. Clothes and Shoes (Fashion)
     3. Writing Instruments
     4. Table Instruments and Decorations
     5. Watches, Jewelry and Silverware
     6. Leather Goods
     7. Wines and Spirits
     8. Gastronomy
     9. Automobiles
     10. Tobacco and Cigarettes

19   See Kaplan's unipolar evaluation in "On the ambivalence-indifference problem in attitude theory and measurement: A suggested modification of the semantic differential technique", *Psychological Bulletin*, 1972, 77, pp. 361–72.

20   This confirmed model is double tested by the Structural Equation Modeling method (AMOS 5). The validity indexes are all satisfactory (Chi-square= 29.210, DF=23, Chi-square/DL= 1.27, RMR=0.073, GFI=0.983, AGFI=0.967, CFI=0.990, RMSEA=0.027). Thus, the general validity of the model is also confirmed.

21   Newby-Clark et al., op. cit.

22   "Conspicuous consumption in China, Luxury's New Empire", *The Economist*, 19 June 2004, p. 65.

How To Succeed In The Chinese Luxury Market[1]

T HE CHINESE MARKET is without doubt the most attractive market in the world. Having gained a deeper understanding of Chinese luxury consumers, the question facing luxury houses now is how they can integrate this understanding into their China market strategies. I conclude this book with the following 10 strategies, some of which are applicable to international brands, some to Asian or Chinese brands, and some to both.

The leading European and U.S. luxury brands have generally been in existence for many years and command very high brand awareness worldwide. They have complete product lines in different categories, and are operated by world-class international management teams. By comparison, Chinese brands such as NE Tiger, Shanghai Tang, and Ports International are just setting out on the luxury road. They lack sophisticated designs, their brands are relatively unknown, their product lines are still developing, and some lack international management expertise and experience. But they know the Chinese market very well and are familiar with Chinese consumers and the way they think.

Common strategies

Strategy 1: Matching consumer needs and product lines

Currently, and for the next few decades, the Chinese luxury market will continue to be dominated by luxury lovers and luxury followers. This means that products such as Louis Vuitton monogram bags, Lacoste polo shirts, Gucci bags, Zegna suits, and Omega and Rolex watches will maintain a strong presence in the market. These are the signature products that have become symbols of social success and the means by which the Chinese *nouveau riche* declare their social status.

However, luxury houses cannot simply focus on these groups: the luxury-intellectual segment will continue to grow and their more sophisticated, less conspicuous, needs represent a strengthening demand for Chinese-rooted luxury tastes and culture.

The strong cultural roots of Chinese luxury consumers will influence the whole luxury industry and push the luxury fashion industry to a higher stage of development, with more sophisticated products, more new technologies, more talented designers, and inspirational design ideas.

Therefore, in order to have sustainable development in the Chinese luxury market, brands should have a rich and complete product portfolio that can fulfill the needs of these three segments of the market, and do so through having product lines that are perfectly consistent with their brand values and house cultures.

Strategy 2: Building a strong brand with effective marketing communication

The image and reputation of a luxury brand are built through having integrated marketing communications geared specifically to the luxury sector, and through selective retailing networks—the boutiques.

Integrated marketing communications

Because of their high-end brand positioning which targets an affluent market, the luxury houses should avoid the usual mass-market communication channels. In any event, the cost of advertising on TV is astronomical and beyond the budget of many. In many people's minds there is a direct link between luxury brands and fashion magazines such as *Elle, Vogue,* and *Cosmopolitan.* In fact, fashion magazines are not an effective approach for luxury brands to reach their targeted market because the readers of such magazines are not the buyers of luxury goods: generally, they are from the lower-middle class or students—that is, people who have a luxury dream and are eager to know luxury brands' legendary stories. While it is a good thing to educate the potential market and to maintain a presence in the fashion media, in itself this is not sufficient to generate direct sales.

The most effective marketing communication strategy for luxury brands is to focus on and invest in high-end lifestyle, cultural, and social magazines (*Yachting, Chinese National Geographic, Sanlian Life Weekly,* for example), financial magazines and management journals (*Financial Times China, Harvard Business Review China* ...), travel and airline magazines available only in the VIP lounge for business and first-class guests, and in the magazines of the major banks.

On the pubic relations side, in addition to the regular fashion shows and product launches, the luxury houses should integrate more cultural and artistic elements into their parties. For example, the most famous luxury party in Beijing was organized by Dunhill, which presented its new collection at the trendy 798, an abandoned factory area now occupied by Chinese artists and home to galleries, restaurants, and cafés. Dunhill invited Cui Jian, the most famous Chinese rock star of the 1980s and '90s, to perform for its successful, middle-aged, male clients and the Harley Davidson club was also present to reinforce the aura of strong masculinity.

Luxury firms should also sponsor elegant artistic and sporting events. (Louis Vuitton has sponsored Asian artists' exhibitions in Beijing and

Hermès organized its Carré design exhibitions in Shanghai.) By becoming associated with such cultural events the luxury brands give consumers and potential consumers an opportunity to have direct personal contact with the brand stories and brand values, taking the relationship beyond the merely commercial. In the sporting world, Lacoste is associated with tennis worldwide and sponsors the two most important international tennis tournaments in China—the China Open in Beijing and the Tennis Masters Cup in Shanghai—creating a very positive image of Lacoste as a high-end French leisure and fashion brand. Rolex and Longines are among many other luxury brands which have adopted similar strategies.

Selective retailing

Having a store in the luxury landmark building or area in the major cities is an unrivaled means of building your brand identity in the market. As Michel Chevalier and Gérald Mazzalovo have pointed out,[2] a luxury brand should be international. If people can find your boutiques in every central business district of every economic hub in the world, your luxury positioning cannot be denied. This rule is also valid in China.

As we have seen, the main landmarks in Shanghai, Beijing, Hangzhou, Guangzhou, and Chengdu are the best locations to build your brand image and reach your targeted clients. Luxury lovers, followers, and intellectuals are all regular visitors to these high-end commercial centers and shopping malls. Investing in your stores is the most direct and effective way to generate sales and build a loyal following.

Ideally, you should have a beautiful flagship store either around Plaza 66 and Shanghai City, or on the Bund area of Shanghai to show to your clients, partners, and market that you are successful in China's most fashionable and international city. But this on its own is not enough. On the back of this, you should then build selective networks in northern China (in Beijing, Shenyang, Dalian, Changchun ...) and in the richest provinces (Zhejiang, Jiangsu, Guangdong, and Fujian). For your PR events, you should find a balance between Beijing and Shanghai, which are both crucial for your business in China.

Strategy 3: Writing your legend, building your story

Only the best products and services can survive in this high-end market. This is the basic yardstick for fashion and luxury houses.

While it may be tempting to think that because the Chinese luxury market has not yet reached the level of sophistication of its U.S. or European counterparts that you can get away with trading on the more superficial side of luxury products; this is completely mistaken. The core market for luxury products is at the top of the social pyramid, the elite, who know the meaning of luxury and are not easily taken in by second-rate products and services.

As we saw earlier, any brand seeking to position itself in the luxury market should be able to show that its products are of excellent quality, a fundamental requirement that some high-end international brands neglect when they enter the Chinese market. Notable among these is the SK-II cosmetics company, which suffered disastrous results when its products failed to meet the standards required by Chinese authorities. Big names such as Prada and Chanel have also been the subject of complaints about poor quality. Such complaints have a direct impact on sales and it takes a very long time to rebuild consumer confidence.

Strategy 4: Hiring talented people with multinational experience and operational effectiveness

This is the most challenging issue facing Chinese and international brands alike. The international brands may have experienced managers with luxury know-how but these people often have no great understanding of the Chinese market. On the other hand, while the Chinese brands have a greater understanding of the local market, they often lack a world-class management team and experience of the luxury industry.

In each case, the solution lies in finding suitably talented people with a multinational background. The perfect profile of a brand or store

manager for a luxury brand in the Chinese market would include the
following attributes:

- A master's degree or an MBA in fashion and luxury brand
  management from a prestigious European business school
- At least two years' luxury-related experience (retailing or PR)
- Spoken fluency in three languages—English, Mandarin, and French
  or Italian—with at least three years' business experience in China
- Strong coordination and implementation abilities.

Managers with a multinational background will have a greater understanding of brand values and culture to ensure the coherence of the brand
identity worldwide, and an understanding of the market to better meet
the needs of clients and follow the trends of the market's evolution.

Strategies for international brands

Because a luxury brand's values and culture are the core characteristics of
a luxury product, international marketing for luxury brands follows a standardized strategy rather than one adapted to local markets. Therefore, the
strategies for international luxury brands in the Chinese market should
seek to balance brand values and local cultures and values.

Strategy 5: Building a strong brand in line with the level
of brand awareness

The branding strategy for luxury brands in a market which has a strong
cultural background should differ according to the levels of brand
awareness in the domestic market. These approaches summarized in
Table 1 below:

TABLE 1: *Branding strategies for developing markets*

Local Market	Luxury Brand Awareness High	Luxury Brand Awareness Low
Local Culture: Strong	1. Integrate more local elements in brand's worldwide identity	3. Continue to build a strong brand with your international identity
Local Culture: Weak	2. Consider the local market as home country and standardize marketing communication	4. Start to build a strong brand with your international identity

International luxury brands, which may already have worldwide brand awareness, should build local brand awareness using the same standardized communication strategy. Because they represent the European and North American cultures, with their high living conditions and excellent quality of production and design, they can be easily accepted by consumers who have a positive attitude toward the Western lifestyle, which is the general trend of the current stage of China's social evolution since Deng's reforms. On the other hand, however, there is the risk that such products will always be seen as exotic and will not be totally accepted by local consumers as representing their own values.

The best way to solve this problem is simply to integrate more Asian values into worldwide marketing communications—using more Asian images in advertising campaigns and more Asian models in fashion shows and press conferences, and inviting Asian artists to develop new product lines.

To overcome strong cultural barriers and realize the great potential that such markets have to offer, the brands should make some compromise between the brand values and local market values through integrating local market elements into their international brand communications and product designs. The worldwide success of Louis Vuitton illustrates the usefulness of such a strategy. To meet the needs of the Japanese market, Louis Vuitton worked with Japanese artist Takashi Murakami in developing the Monogram Multicolor canvas for its Spring–Summer 2003 show, and this is now a permanent line worldwide. In addition, in 2007, it invited Du Juan, a top Chinese model, to join its worldwide advertising campaign, integrating an Asian face into its worldwide communications.

The Olympic Games in Beijing and the World Expo in Shanghai will ensure that the world's gaze is focused on China, providing ideal opportunities for brands to demonstrate their strength in the world's most dynamic market. Zegna's 2008 worldwide advertising is organized against the background of the Olympic Games and China's vibrant market. Such strategies can create strong attachments with Asian consumers, helping them to feel comfortable enough to accept the brands and their cultures as their own.

Sponsoring various cultural and artistic events is an effective gesture to show the respect for Chinese culture which is crucial for doing business in China, as we noted in earlier chapters. Becoming involved in and associated with local cultural activities creates a positive image in consumers' minds, which can then generate sales and market share.

In places such as Singapore and Hong Kong, which are international cities in their own right and where the Chinese cultural aspect is perhaps not as strong, any branding strategy should be the same as that used in the brands' home countries.

Strategy 6: Determining market entrance strategy according to the company's business model, its brand awareness in the local market, and its understanding of that market

The entrance strategy is always the most important decision facing international brands about to enter any market.

Each brand has its own business model and international distribution strategies, and China is a very complicated market. The correct approach to use will depend on several factors: your brand awareness in the local market, your capital and cash-flow situation, your understanding of the market, and the strength of your local partner. The various strategies are summarized in the following table.

TABLE 2: *Market entrance strategies for the China luxury market*

Choice for Market Entrance	Brand Awareness in Local Market	Capital/ Cash-flow Requirements	Understanding of the Market	Strength of Local Partner
Exclusive Sales in Home Country	Middle	Low	Low	High
Subsidiaries	High	High	High	N/A
Local Distribution	Low/Middle	Low	Low	High
Joint Venture	High	Middle	Middle	High/Middle

Chevalier and Mazzalovo have identified four main methods by which luxury brands can distribute their products worldwide: through exclusive sales in the local, home country market; through subsidiaries; through local distributors; and through joint ventures.[3]

Having exclusive sales in the local market is the method used by fashion and luxury brands to start their business. Under this system, powerful department stores from the U.S., Japan, and Korea send representatives to fashion weeks (organized by fashion and luxury brands to show their new collections to key clients, the fashion media, and the public) to make their orders for the following year. But this model is not suitable for the China market because the Chinese department stores are not strong enough to organize their own sales and choose brands. The role they play is solely that of landlords and is confined to welcoming luxury brands to set up shop-in-shop arrangements in their mall. It would be wiser, therefore, to choose either subsidiaries or local distributors, or to create a joint venture with a local partner.

How to start a luxury business in China

For a luxury brand with very high brand awareness worldwide and with sufficient capital and cash flow to ensure an investment of between three and five years, there are two possibilities for establishing a local presence. Assuming a reasonable understanding of the Chinese market, the best strategy is to create a subsidiary with 100%-owned stores in every targeted city, because the luxury market will boom in the long term and Chinese consumers have sufficient buying power to make the investment profit-able within a couple of years. In 2004, Patek Philippe opened its first Asian store on the Bund in Shanghai. Several times during the following two years, its classic models displayed in the window were sold out. At the end of 2007, another store opened in Beijing.

For those less familiar with the Chinese market, a second possibility is to create a joint venture with a powerful local distributor of luxury goods. The chosen distributor will be able to share local knowledge, help set up a distribution network in the right places, and use the most effective local media to communicate and build local brand awareness.

Many of the big luxury brands began their distribution in China in this way, and many (including Dunhill) used the influential China Resources Group as their local distributor. LVMH also started its Chinese ventures through a distributor (Bluebell of Hong Kong). After 1992, LVMH changed its strategies and created joint ventures with Bluebell (for Louis Vuitton and Loewe products) and with Riche Monde (for wines and spirits). At that time, Chinese regulations did not allow foreign companies to distribute imported products directly. However, since China joined the WTO these restrictions have been relaxed and, in 2005, LVMH started to buy back all the rights and to handle the distribution itself. From 2007, 100% foreign-capital companies can sell all imported and Chinese products. Sephora entered the market in 2005. Christian Dior set up a subsidiary to handle the perfumes business. Some of the LVMH brands, including Givenchy, are still distributed by franchise.

Where capital and cash-flow constraints do not allow a brand to create a subsidiary, the best strategy is to find a powerful local distributor to handle distribution in China. While this will bring the benefit of local knowledge, it also means that the brand does not have complete control of its brand image and communication in the market. This is the case for many brands—Givenchy, Cerruti 1881, Valentino, Pierre Cardin, Lancel, and Longchamps, to name but a few.

For a luxury brand with middle or low brand awareness in the world-wide market, where capital and cash flow allow, the best strategy is to create a joint venture with a powerful local distributor to develop the business and build strong brand awareness with an international identity in the local market.

Those that know the local market well can set up their own wholly owned stores. As we saw earlier, before its entry into the China market the brand awareness of the Canadian fashion brand Ports International was limited to North America. However, the Chan family's deeper understanding of the Chinese market enabled it to create its own retailing networks in Shanghai and Xiamen. This strategy proved to be appropriate and very effective, helping Ports to create very strong local brand awareness with an international identity, and generate massive sales.

For new luxury brands, with only limited levels of awareness in Europe and the U.S. and limited capital for investment, the best strategy is to find a distributor to develop the business and build brand awareness locally. What the brands lose in control, they gain in having a presence in China. Take, for example, the case of Foli Folie, the Greek lifestyle accessory brand. When it entered the Chinese market in 2002, very few people knew this brand. But by 2007, its Chinese distributor, Pilion Trading Co. Ltd, had set up more than 40 stores in 23 cities and provinces. Because of the design and middle-end positioning and pricing strategy, Foli Folie has become very popular and widely accepted by Chinese consumers.

Strategy 7: Expanding presence in China

The majority of the international luxury brands in China started their business through local distributors—in Hong Kong, Taiwan, and the Mainland itself. Many (Lacoste, Louis Vuitton, Zegna, and Cartier, for example) came into the market in the late 1980s and early 1990s. Other brands, principally the watch brands such as Omega, Rolex, and Rado, entered even earlier. Aware that they were taking a big risk in an unstable market, these early movers also realized the huge potential of the market. Because they were very obvious and rare in the Chinese market, and although very few could actually afford to buy their products, these brands were able to create strong brand awareness.

However, now that they are well established, they face fresh challenges over how best to take advantage of the luxury boom in China. Should they continue with the same distribution structure as when they first entered the market? What are the best strategies to ensure rapid and effective expansion in the Chinese luxury market?

For these brands, the distribution networks which served them well in the early years may no longer be suitable for further expansion. The main objective of distributors is not to promote the brand image, but the revenues and the margins they can keep for themselves. But for luxury brands, the sales volumes have already attained a level that allows them to set up subsidiaries and, more importantly, they need to have direct control in order to maintain the consistency of the brand's image worldwide.

The best strategy for this second stage of development in China, therefore, is for the brands to buy back the distribution rights from their licensed distributors. This is precisely what the likes of Dunhill, Zegna, and Valentino have done in order to handle the Mainland market themselves.

After gaining direct control of the distribution network, the brands then need to embark on massive—though carefully controlled—expansion (see Strategy 2 above).

Expansion through merger and acquisition

The current situation in the Chinese luxury market is that market development is outpacing the opening of new luxury stores. It is hard to open new stores in strategic cities, so the luxury brands should be looking to expand into second-tier cities. However, the necessary infrastructure for selective retailing in these cities is not always what it should be. In these circumstances, the luxury brands would be well advised to acquire some Chinese brands with a good image and development potential.

The first company to adopt such a strategy was L'Oréal. After eight years of development in China, L'Oréal acquired two Chinese brands, Mini Nurse and Yu Sai, in 2004. These brands have helped L'Oréal to establish itself in the middle- and high-end skin-care and cosmetics market. The same strategy was also adopted by the Richemont group, which acquired the Hong Kong fashion brand Shanghai Tang, whose Asian operations represent 80% of its global sales. In 2005, the group's overall sales in Asia (outside of Japan) grew 20%, compared to 10% in Europe, 7% in the Americas, and 3% in Japan.

LVMH is also extremely active in this field. In 2007, it invested US$30 million in Belle International, the first distributor of LVMH women's shoes in China. This Chinese group owns more than 3,700 shops in China, where its market share is estimated at 8.2%. It also has 35 shops in Hong Kong, in Macao, and in the United States. The group is also one of the most important distributors of sports products and brands in China, including Nike products.

Strategies for developing Chinese luxury brands

Strategy 8: Going international to build a luxury identity

To be a real luxury brand in the 21st century requires three basic conditions: craftsmanship, products that are aesthetically appealing, and an international profile.

The first two conditions are fundamental for any luxury brand. The third condition is more important and meaningful for a Chinese brand if it is to succeed in the Chinese and worldwide markets. Going international is vital for Chinese companies to acquire a massive domestic market: acceptance by the international market indicates that the quality and design of the Chinese brand have achieved a real world-class level. Having international recognition breeds confidence among the Chinese brands and consumers alike.

For example, in 2000, Hair, a Chinese home-appliance company, realized that in an era of globalization it would have to learn how to compete with General Electric and Whirlpool on their home turf; otherwise, it would lose its Chinese market. Hair understood that in order to succeed in easier markets, it first had to penetrate the difficult markets of the United States and Europe. Chinese fashion brands all face the same problem: self-confidence. The only way to solve the problem is to go international to acquire the recognition of the world.

Strategy 9: Chinese elements alone are not enough

As we saw with the examples of NE Tiger and Shanghai Tang, for Chinese fashion brands Chinese elements are surely the most important roots from which come the inspiration and imagination of the designers. However, in order to be accepted on the world market, where the fashion world changes so fast and consumers are impatient for new trends and new elements, something more than Chinese elements is required.

Thus, in addition to Chinese-oriented collections, multi-collections or international collections should also be introduced into each new season's fashion shows. This isn't easy, because it requires designers with the talent and energy to deliver products that can please both domestic and international consumers. In this regard, Chinese fashion brands still have a long way to go.

Strategy 10: Repositioning the brand

In the Chinese luxury market, there are several Chinese brands with a very traditional image, especially in the jewelry sector. Xie Ruilin and Zhou Sengseng are Hong Kong-based jewelry brands which, because of their long history and good-quality products, command very high awareness among senior consumers and the low-end market. However, their designs and management cannot compete with international jewelry brands such as Cartier, Boucheron, and Van Cleef & Arpels.

For Chinese brands to be able to compete in the international market will require that they reposition themselves. To do this, they should build an international management team and work with world-class experts in luxury branding. This is a challenge for brand owners because such fundamental changes are not easily accepted by those who have been responsible for putting the brand in its current position.

As part of those changes, it is also vital to work with world-class designers with avant-garde design concepts. In concept development and design, there can be no compromise: everything should be perfect before launching into the market. Every piece should convey uniqueness and elegance.

Branding is both a marketing strategy and an art. Before you start to build, you should be clear about your brand identity and how you want consumers to perceive your brand. You should know your ideal positioning through market analysis and, should this prove to be problematic, luxury branding experts can be called in to conduct a brand audit and make a complete branding plan with detailed communication and marketing action.

For some brands, it will be a case of improving their retailing networks. This might entail opening flagship stores in luxury landmarks and canceling retailing outlets in low-end locations, even if these are very profitable. It is a very tough job for brands to improve their image by cutting cash cows. But for a brand's long-term development, this is vital. Otherwise, all the hard work in branding, working with designers, and recruiting an international team will be a waste of money.

ENDNOTES

1   Written with Bernard Pras, Professor of Marketing , University of Paris Dauphine and Essec.
2   See *Luxury Brand Management*, John Wiley & Sons, 2008.
3   Ibid.

F ROM THE RESULTS of the cluster analysis based on the psychographic traits and the variations in their luxury consumption behavior, the profiles of the four Chinese luxury consumer groups became clearer and more detailed. A discriminant analysis was then conducted to illustrate the direct relations between them. (Discriminant analysis is a technique for classifying a set of observations into predefined classes. The purpose is to determine the class of an observation based on a set of variables known as "predictors" or "input variables." The model is built on a set of observations for which the classes are known. This set of observations is sometimes referred to as the "training set." Based on the training set, the technique constructs a set of linear functions of the predictors, known as "discriminant functions.")

The within-groups results showed that the correlations between the variables are very low. The equality of group means is significant (at 0.001 in all cases), but for post-purchase guilt and innovativeness, significant levels are at 0.025 and 0.007, respectively.

TABLE A1: *Result of the discriminant analysis (mean)*

Mean	Indivi-dualist	Conspi-cuous	Impulsive	Brand Loyalty	Post-Purchase Guilt	Innova-tiveness
Lovers	−0.40034	1.00190	−0.49517	−0.51634	−0.31908	0.25807
Followers	−0.98137	0.48361	0.57868	−0.11528	0.23295	0.15312
Intellectuals	0.71171	−0.06478	−0.69770	0.08299	0.04627	0.01623
Laggards	0.09115	−0.85368	0.70441	0.27043	−0.06774	−0.28453

TABLE A2: *Result of the discriminant analysis (standard deviation)*

Std. Deviation	Indivi-dualist	Conspi-cuous	Impulsive	Brand Loyalty	Post-Purchase Guilt	Innova-tiveness
Lovers	0.93849	0.76407	0.93389	0.98584	1.05345	1.04223
Followers	0.75649	0.78916	0.68116	0.95297	0.92769	0.96533
Intellectuals	0.52693	0.76293	0.77091	1.04970	0.94018	1.01280
Laggards	0.91533	0.77755	0.71535	0.86617	1.06104	0.93297

From the structure matrix, the result showed that modern individualist and impulsiveness have the strongest correlations with discriminant function 1; and conspicuousness and innovativeness have the strongest correlations with discriminant function 2; and finally, post-purchase guilt and brand loyalty are strongly correlated to discriminant function 3 whose Wilk's λ is not significant.

In terms of the validity of the classification, Table A3 shows that for luxury lovers, the rate of error is 0%: for the followers, 10 cases were misclassified as lovers and four as laggards, with misclassification rates of 14.5% and 5.8%, respectively. For intellectuals, three cases were misclassified as lovers and four as laggards, the misclassification rates being 2.7% and 3.6%, respectively. For the laggards, two cases were misclassified as followers, for a misclassification rate of 2.3%.

The correct classification rate of the total sample is 92.7% of the original grouped cases. Thus, the conclusion can be drawn that this classification is validated and the segmentation from the propositions appear to be sound.

TABLE A3: *Classification result of the discriminant analysis*

CHINESE LUXURY CONSUMER MARKET			Predicted Group Membership				Total
			Lovers	Followers	Intellectuals	Laggards	
Original	Count	Lovers	48	0	0	0	48
		Followers	10	55	0	4	69
		Intellectuals	3	0	104	4	111
		Laggards	0	2	0	85	87
	%	Lovers	100.0	.0	.0	.0	100.0
		Followers	14.5	79.7	.0	5.8	100.0
		Intellectuals	2.7	.0	93.7	3.6	100.0
		Laggards	.0	2.3	.0	97.7	100.0

FIGURE A1: *Canonical discriminant functions graph*

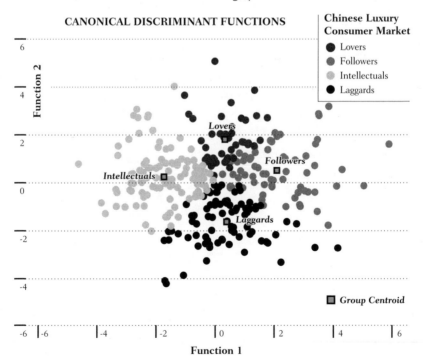

The discriminant analysis confirmed the results of the cluster analysis, clarifying the general vision of the four segments. With the six psychographic and consumption variables, Fisher's linear discriminant functions were found. The coefficients were calculated and the result was confirmed by the validity analysis.

The results showed that the modern individualist and impulsiveness are significantly correlated. There was a strong correlation too between conspicuousness and innovativeness.

The first correlation between individualism and impulsiveness explains the illogicality of the lovers' negative values toward the modern individualist factor and the impulsiveness factor. After combining the two variables to create a new variable—impulsive * individualist—the analysis of variance showed that the lovers reported the highest value among the four groups with a positive value; the laggards reported the second-highest value, also positive. However, the high scores have different causes: the luxury lovers are mostly rational and collective and the luxury laggards are rather impulsive (except upon price, as mentioned earlier) and rather individualist.

ANOVA—analysis of variance 015 (a collection of statistical models, and their associated procedures, in which the observed variance is partitioned into components due to different explanatory variables)

Impulsive * Individualist

TABLE A4: *Analysis of variance, dependent variable: impulsive * individualist*

	Sum of Squares	df	Mean Square	F	Sig.
Between Groups	82.257	3	27.419	29.565	.000
Within Groups	288.426	311	.927		
Total	370.683	314			

FIGURE A2: *The Analysis of Variance of the Impulsive * Individualist*

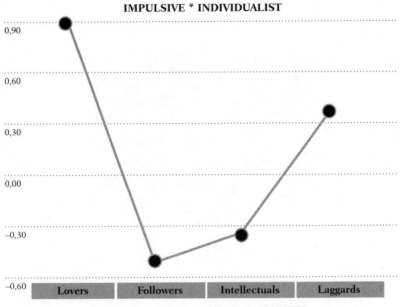

IMPULSIVE * INDIVIDUALIST

CHINESE LUXURY CONSUMER MARKET

The second correlation between conspicuousness and innovativeness explains that the innovativeness of the luxury product is a key element in boosting the conspicuousness effect of such products. These results reflect the reality within the luxury industry. The luxury firms launch new collections every six months to sustain innovation. On the one hand, the new collections lead the fashion trend of the season; on the other, the innovativeness generated by new models and new products maintains the conspicuousness of the luxury brand that attracts the luxury consumers sensitive to conspicuousness. This point is confirmed by the rapid worldwide success of fast-fashion brands such as Zara and H&M, which accelerated the whole fashion industry by shortening the period between the two seasons through launching small collections and special collections during the period.

Thus, the proposed matrix of segmentation based on the qualitative study should be adjusted as follows:

FIGURE A3: *The adjusted segmentation matrix: Individualist/Impulsive*

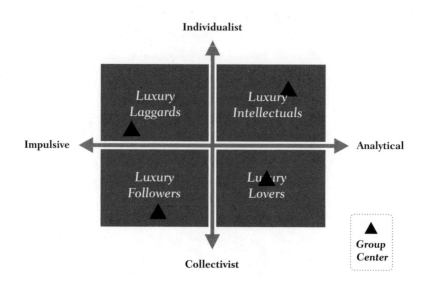

There are no significant changes in the first proposed matrix. However, in the second matrix (compared to Figure 4.2), the individualist vs. collectivist/conspicuous vs. functional, the distribution of the four segments does not equilibrate. The luxury intellectuals and the laggards are situated at the same time in the individualist and functional quadrant; the luxury lovers and the followers are situated in the conspicuous and collectivist quadrant. The degree of the conspicuousness and the functionality of the four segments are not the same; thus, the distribution of the four segments on this factor can be clearly distinguished. However, there are two empty quadrants in the matrix. This means that there are no, or very few, Chinese luxury consumers who have the profile described by the two factors of the matrix: the conspicuous individualist and the functional collectivist.

The results are logical considering the motivations for buying luxury goods in Chinese society shown in Chapter 1. Conspicuousness is linked with the social awareness of the individual; for example, to buy conspicuous luxury goods in order to show wealth and success in front of friends,

FIGURE A4: *The adjusted segmentation matrix: Individualist/Conspicuous*

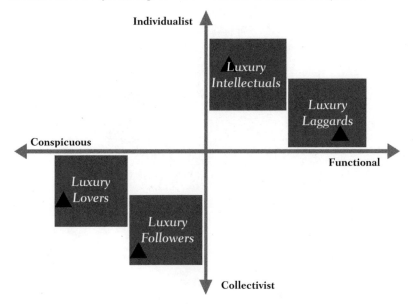

colleagues, and other people. Thus, the conspicuous consumers are collectivist too.

The functional collectivists are also very few among Chinese luxury consumers. This result is logical as well, because of the special characteristics of the products involved: luxury goods. Functional luxury consumers choose certain luxury goods in order to fulfill functional needs such as the very act of possession. Therefore, they often ignore the conspicuousness of the product, but focus on the excellent quality and sophisticated design. Thus, their choice involves fewer social considerations, such as the desire to show off. They are consequently functional individualists. For example, as we saw, a Chinese consumer of a Rolex and a Chinese consumer of a Breguet have completely different mentality and motivation for their luxury consumption: one buys Rolex for conspicuousness; the other buys Breguet for more personal reasons based on the happiness that possession brings.